# The Birds of Virginia's Colonial Historic Triangle

## An annotated checklist

**Edited by Bill Williams**

*Book design and layout by Louise Menges*
*Cover photo by Mike Powell*
*Williamsburg Bird Club logo on back cover from an original design by Rich Goll*
*Title page photo by Joe Piotrowski*

ISBN: 978-0-615-70841-6

# Table of Contents

# Introduction

*"Curlews and whimbrels have a general similarity, and both have two wings; yet to any but the most superficial observer there is an evident difference … The accustomed eye … at once distinguishes the equivalent of eye-stripes, wing-bars and semi-palmated feet."*

Dr. Stephem Maturin to Reverend Nathaniel Martin
from *The Letter of Marque* by Patrick O'Brian

The Williamsburg Bird Club published *Birds of the Williamsburg Area: An Annotated Checklist* in May 1998 to commemorate the club's 1997 twentieth anniversary. That publication, edited by William J. Sheehan, then the bird club's Records Committee chairman, synthesized much of the recorded information for the 326 bird species that had been documented within the Colonial Historic Triangle (James City County, City of Williamsburg, York County, and Hog Island Wildlife Management Area, Surry County) through 1997. Since then additional information regarding the area's birdlife has come to light, the result of more detailed analysis of the historical record and the increased number and sophistication of observers with their rapidly evolving technology through which sightings can be communicated and verified.

This publication annotates the status of 346 species that have been verified in the Colonial Historic Triangle through September 30, 2012. Included among this total are two extinct species, Passenger Pigeon and Carolina Parakeet, and 9 introduced/exotic species: Mute Swan, Barnacle Goose, Ring-necked Pheasant, Rock Pigeon, African Collared-Dove, European Starling, House Finch, European Goldfinch, and House Sparrow. Records for White-tailed Kite, Fork-tailed Flycatcher, and Shiny Cowbird merited inclusion herein as each was discovered within close proximity to the Colonial Historic Triangle's jurisdictional boundaries. The local occurrence of two subspecies, Audubon's Yellow-rumped Warbler, and Ipswich Savannah Sparrow are detailed, as are those of 4 hybrids, Mallard × American Black Duck, Brewster's Warbler, Lawrence's Warbler, and White-throated Sparrow × Dark-eyed Junco. To date 117 species are known to breed or were known to have bred in the Colonial Historic Triangle. Another 8 species are (or were) probable local breeders, including Northern Shoveler, Sharp-shinned Hawk, Chuck-will's-widow, Whip-poor-will, Loggerhead Shrike, Worm-eating Warbler, Yellow Warbler, and American Goldfinch.

The **Species Accounts** details validate the Colonial Historic Triangle's preeminence in Virginia's ornithology. The area can lay claim to the Commonwealth's first confirmed Virginia records for Western/Clark's Grebe, nesting Anhinga, White-tailed Kite, Fork-tailed Flycatcher, Spotted Towhee, wintering Dickcissel, and Shiny Cowbird, and was among the first to record Fulvous Whistling-Duck. The state's second confirmed Northern Shrike and Townsend's Solitaire and third Townsend's Warbler were in "Williamsburg." The Williamsburg Christmas Bird Count had the 1980–81 CBC season national high count of 15 Baltimore Orioles on December 21, 1980.

The annotations applied in this document are, by their very nature, statements of history. As such, some will be out of date before the publication fledges. When viewed in the context of this region's historic past the stories told by these records are testament to the people who recorded them and the places where the birds were encountered.

The **Species Accounts** nomenclature and taxonomic order are those of the American Ornithologists' Union through July 2012. Errors of substance and subjectivity for this current iteration of the Colonial Historic Triangle's bird records are the full responsibility of the editor. Annotated checklists are bound to be bested. In that capacity they fulfill their purposes of synthesizing current knowledge, promoting skepticism, and encouraging more diligent field observation, record keeping, and accurate documentation. Without such ongoing refinement the true nature of the local avifauna tracks a course of misinformed speculation.

# Acknowledgements

Bill Sheehan worked for more than 20 years to compile and meticulously organize myriads of local bird records from the late 1970s into 1999. His extensive notebooks of current and historical data for each species served as the foundation for this current annotated checklist. Good on you, Sheehan.

The layout and organization of this book were in the best of hands. Louise Menges' patient attention to quality and precision brought this work to life. Her practiced eye for design and flow assured every letter and punctuation mark was correct. The success of that effort is readily apparent. Fred Blystone's careful examination of the text and photos proved invaluable. Tom Armour, Hugh Beard, and Brian Taber reviewed the initial species accounts drafts. Shirley Devan and Jeanette Navia edited the final text with exceptional precision and care. Mark Rinaldi's deft handiwork rendered the Colonial Historic Triangle map.

Dr. Joanne Bowen, Curator of Zoology; Archaeological Research for The Colonial Williamsburg Foundation cannot be thanked enough for her erudite contributions to understandings of the colonial period's foodways systems and how these influenced the Colonial Historic Triangle's changing landscape. Alain Outlaw, Jim Dorsey, and Sara Lewis provided valuable insights into the cultural dynamics which impacted local flora and fauna throughout colonial times. Dr. Stewart Ware was immensely helpful with his empirical evidence of the history of change to the southeastern hardwood forests. Dr. Gerald (Jerre) Johnson enthusiastically made the local geology a thing of the present.

It would be hard to quantify much less adequately express enough gratitude for the guidance and friendship Dr. Mitchell Byrd has so unselfishly given to so many bird enthusiasts for more than six decades. Likewise, Ruth Beck's generous dedication and willingness to coach and share have made a world of difference to "the bird people" for more than 40 years.

Dr. Bryan Watts, Director of the Center for Conservation Biology at the College of William and Mary/Virginia Commonwealth University made available technical reports and master's of arts theses that linked annotations with protocol driven research.

Dr. Adam Duerr shared his knowledge about Black Vulture dispersal and Scott Lerberg of the Chesapeake Bay National Estuarine Research Reserve at the Virginia Institute of Marine Science ferreted out critical lower York County avian monitoring project reports.

Far and away the most sincere huzzahs are for those folks who posted and continue to post their bird sightings to the Williamsburg Bird Club.

# An Historic Context

The naturalist in each of us is compelled to idealize the scope and diversity of the flora and fauna that were presented to the New World founders as they made their initial forays into the region. Those who explored the environs of the present-day Colonial Historic Triangle in the mid 16th century and those who settled the area shortly after the turn of the 17th century entered a landscape that had been manipulated by human endeavors for centuries. The seemingly lush forests, pristine waterways, and apparent abundance of wildlife stood in stark contrast to the highly developed landscape and depleted natural resources of the 17th century Europe from which the arriving entrepreneurs emigrated. The eloquent diaries of John Smith, William Strachey, Durand de Dauphine, Francis Nicholson, John White, John Lawson, and others bear witness to the colonists' high expectations for their perceived New World cornucopia. Those documentaries captured the first insights into the region's avifauna, accounts which have been synthesized into the ornithological record by many authors. As significant and enticing as those anecdotes were, they foundered by default, as an acknowledged avian nomenclature system was more than a century in the offing. Early writers therefore applied names to bird species based on their resemblance to European cognates or on their obvious vocal and/or morphological characteristics. That birds were viewed, first and foremost, as a necessary and readily available food source, much of what was recorded about them was biased by their value as table fare. It must also be recognized that the subjective rhetoric of those first avian annotations, as revealing and genuine as they seemed, were often framed by more than a modicum of hyperbole scripted to promote further New World exploration and investment.

> There is a prodigous quantity of birds. Beginning with the largest, the wild turkeys weigh from 30 to 40 pounds. One sees on the shores of the sea and on the banks of the rivers wild geese in troupes of more than 4,000 at a time. They are as big as our domestic geese, but almost black. Ducks appear in flocks of more than 10,000. There are also doves and thrushes. Partridges are so plentiful and so tame that they come into the barnyards. They are smaller than those of Europe, but of the same taste. All these birds have different plumage from ours in Europe; indeed, I saw none of similar plumage except the crows and black birds. There are quantities of shore birds available for game, but the hunters despise them and never even waste powder on the ducks unless assured of killing three or four at a shot.
>
> Durand de Dauphine, 1686.

Fortunately, archaeological investigations have fashioned an empirical bridge from those early settlement times to the present. Analyses of foodways debris excavated from Jamestown trash pits dating to 1610 provide modern-day taxonomic validation for the occurrence of some of the avifauna that were present locally four centuries ago. Among the taxa cataloged from the refuse are: Domestic Goose, Canada Goose, Wood Duck, American Black Duck, Mallard or domestic Duck, Ring-necked Duck, *Aythya sp.*, Ruddy Duck, Chicken, Turkey, Northern Bobwhite, Common Loon, Bermuda Petrel, Double-crested Cormorant, Great Blue Heron, Bald Eagle, *Buteo sp.*, Killdeer, Ring-billed Gull, Family Strigidae, Family Picidae, American Crow, and unidentified perching bird, Order Passeriformes. Surprisingly absent from this list are pigeons and doves despite considerable evidence colonists knew Mourning Doves and Passenger Pigeons well.

> As for pigeons, I saw them only on the plantations of the gentlemen. The peasants despise such small game.
>
> Durand de Dauphine, 1686.

Our understanding of the distribution of modern bird populations suggests with some degree of certainty the species listed above were likely acquired locally. The Bermuda Petrel hovers as the ominous exception, indicative of a harvest pressure on this species that contributed to its presumed extinction by 1621.

Letters of correspondence and inventories of record reveal that birds were valued not only for culinary use but for the economic benefit derived from collecting and selling them for aesthetic purposes locally and for shipment back to the Old World. Francis Nicholson responding to a request from King William posted this 1698 notice:

> "His most Sacred Majesty hath been pleased to signify his royal pleasure to me by $y^e$ right Hon$^{ble}$ Wm. Blaithwait Esqr. & $y^t$ he would have some mocking birds, read-birds, & as also blew-birds, Baltimore-birds, black birds, with red upon their Wings; and any other sort of small birds $y^t$ are curious either for colours, or singing: partridges, pheasants, wild Turkeys, and any other such sot of Fowl; Summer ducks, fishing Hawks, or any other sort of Hawks, Bald Eagles, and all sorts of eagles". Transport cages were provided "with suitable Diet, and other conveniences: and not too many of them together, nor on board ship."

The 1769–1770 Governor's Palace account books list among fauna assembled there …"hummingbird, mockingbird, partridge, red bird, swan, hawk, teal, shelldrakes, turkey, wild duck, wild fowl, wild goose"… several of which were certainly not harvested merely to please the palate.

In the case of the hummingbird the following is particularly intriguing:

> There are also numbers of small forest birds such as we have in Europe. Some, as big as swallows, are entirely red; others, the size of sparrows, all blue; others, not larger than a big fly, have a plumage like the rainbow. This little bird lives only on dew and the nectar of the odoriferous flowers. It has itself so agreeable an odor that they told me the English prize them highly for that quality, wherefore the Virginians dry them in the ovens and sell them in England at a price of eight pounds sterling apiece.
>
> Durand de Dauphine, 1686.

## The Changing Land

Human settlement from the colonial period forward with its concomitant commercial tree harvest, small farms, and large plantations accelerated domestication of the land, primary evidence for which is derived from artist and mapmaker renderings merged with the chronicles of businessmen, land lords and explorers. How avian populations responded to the increasingly fragmented landscape is best conjectured through what is currently understood about how comparable land use practices affect them today. As cultivated soils became nutrient exhausted, more land was cleared, leaving fallow fields and secondary growth to the regenerative progressions of ecological succession. Indeed, within a generation of the earliest settlements laws were enacted to permit fencing designed to keep livestock out rather than in. Free ranging horses and cattle proliferated to such an extent that hunting them was considered sport. Feral pigs became so numerous their foraging has been implicated in the eradication of the longleaf pine throughout the southeast.

By the mid-eighteenth century crop diversification defined the region's landscape mosaic, including, among other entrepreneurial endeavors, attempted rice farming at Green Spring Plantation, part of the current Governor's Land Archaeological District. As the local human population grew and expanded westward so too did the consumptive pressure on wildlife. A 1727 Act to Prevent the Destruction of Wild Fowl, which carried a 20 shilling fine for violators, strongly suggests how deleterious overharvesting of some avian populations had become, especially within the context of the degenerative land exploitations outlined above.

Careful examination of mid to late 19th century Colonial Historic Triangle photographs reveals viewsheds sparsely populated by trees, echoes of the prevalence of farmland and the parallel depletion of forests that characterized the pre-, and especially, the post-Civil War eras well into early 1900s. The 1930 National Agriculture Statistics Service (NASS) report documented that of the 167,108 acres of land in the James City County, York County and the City of Williamsburg complex, 86,130 acres, or 52% of the total acreage, were occupied by 1,068 farms. That rural agrarian character, with its patchworks of open land, fragmented forests and well defined tree-lined borders, continued locally through the 1950s. The 1964 NASS census reported there were 226 farms utilizing 35,505 acres of farmland, 21% of the tri-jurisdictional acreage. The most recent NASS accounting in 2007 showed there were 119 farms on 7,131 acres, a 90% decline in the number of farms and a 92% decline in the amount of land devoted to farming since 1930.

Not unexpectedly, this redirection of land use expressed itself demographically. The Colonial Historic Triangle's population increased from 116,397 in 2000 to 146,541 by 2011, a 26% increase, twice the percentage increase for all of Virginia during the same period. Indeed, James City County was acknowledged to be the fifth fastest growing community in the Commonwealth, a trend likely to continue in view of the projected build-out of 3,600 more homes over the next 20 years in just one residential development in the county's northwest corner.

Positively influencing the impacts on natural systems these challenging population and land use changes portend is that almost 67,000 acres (40%) of the Colonial Historic Triangle's land are protected as federal, state, local, and private holdings. Combined federal lands, military, and national park properties account for approximately 32,000 acres of this total. State managed facilities, among them York River State Park (2,550 acres), the Hog Island Tract of the Hog Island

Wildlife Management Area in Surry County (2,308 acres), and the Grafton Ponds Natural Area Preserve (325 acres) complement locally protected public lands such as Waller Mill Park (2,705 acres), the College of William and Mary Woods (900 acres), Freedom Park (600 acres), and New Quarter Park (545 acres). The Williamsburg Land Conservancy currently holds permanent conservation easements on 1,534 acres of mostly private land in the Colonial Historic Triangle. Thousands of additional acres are protected as watershed buffers around municipal waterworks, as designated green space in local communities and as Resource Protection Areas under the Chesapeake Bay Preservation Act.

The data recounted within this publication span more than 80 years from the early 1930s to the present. They capture a window in time during which permanent changes to the water and landscape systems were promulgated. As much as the European settlement of this region restructured international geopolitical systems, so too did subsequent settlement restructure the face of the Colonial Historic Triangle's flora and fauna. The day-to-day, season-to-season mobility of birds in and of themselves is compelling enough to bring unusual and unprecedented avifauna to our community at almost any moment. As exciting as those fleeting occurrences are, their relevance is overshadowed by the larger issues associated with the long-term, in some cases permanent, elimination of places birds, and all of the interrelated systems necessary to support them, require. Unlike prior decades which witnessed land use transition from farming to timber harvest to slow regeneration, land is now being put to uses that are, for all intents and purposes, irreversible for any type of natural systems that fauna and flora find accommodating, much less sustainable. Effective land management designed for the best circumstances for wildlife diversity within the greater Colonial Historical Triangle has become marginalized at best. Neighborhood patches of vegetation, storm-water ponds and open space offer incoherent whispers of the stories once told within the balanced interplay of fields, forests, and naturally sustained waterways that dominated the Colonial Historic Triangle's previous landscape character.

# Physical Description of Virginia's Colonial Historic Triangle

Virginia's Colonial Historic Triangle—James City County, the City of Williamsburg, York County, and, for the purposes of this publication, the Hog Island Tract of the Hog Island Wildlife Management Area in Surry County—occupies the northern four fifths of the northwest-to-southeast oriented Virginia Peninsula, part of the tidewater region of the Commonwealth's inner Coastal Plain. Bounded on the north by the York River, to the south by the James River, and to the northwest by the Chickahominy River, a tributary of the James, the Triangle's 404.7 mi² area includes a land mass of 257.5 mi² and 147.2 mi² of tidal water that is bordered by 359 miles of estuarine shoreline. Climatologically the region is humid subtropical. The annual mean temperature is 60° F (16° C) with January, the coldest month, averaging 39° F (4° C) and July, the warmest month, averaging 78° F (26° C). The area receives an annual average rainfall of 44 inches and 6–7 inches of snow.

The geomorphology of the Colonial Historic Triangle has been and continues to be determined by its dynamic aquatic systems. Its topography consists of a series of broad, flat terraces that descend from an elevation of 149 feet above sea level in the northwest to 0 feet at the water's edge of the James, York, and Chickahominy rivers. Each scarp of a descending terrace represents an ancient shoreline adjacent to a flat, abandoned river bottom or shallow sea. Sedimentation more than 1000 feet deep in the northwest slopes eastward over a bed of metamorphic rock that is 200 million to 1 billion years old. This highly erodible sediment has been bisected over time by numerous creeks and streams that drain their respective watersheds. The relatively horizontal spine of the peninsula delineates the present-day path of Interstate 64. The City of Williamsburg, centrally located within the Triangle between the James and York rivers, was historically connected to the former by College Creek (once known as Archer's Hope Creek) and to the latter by Queens Creek. In addition to naturally occurring water systems there are five manmade reservoirs within the Colonial Historic Triangle (Bethel, Harwood's Mill, Waller Mill, Diascund, and Little Creek), more than 1000 storm water retention ponds, and numerous former mill and farm ponds.

## Wetland Communities

The Virginia Peninsula has a panoply of estuarine and palustrine wetlands, each an expression of its ecological responses to variations in elevation, hydroperiod, and/or salinity gradients. The York River at its southeast origin is polyhaline (18–30 ppt) from the Goodwin Islands (see **Birding Locations**) to Yorktown, where it becomes mesohaline (5–18 ppt) past York River State Park (see **Birding Locations**). The Goodwin Islands' perimeter dunes support a salt scrub community dominated by groundsel tree (*Baccharis halimifolia*) interspersed with marsh elder (*Iva frutescens*) and saltmeadow hay (*Spartina patens*). American Oystercatchers, Willets, Seaside Sparrows, and Boat-tailed Grackles are encountered during the breeding season in this maritime dune grassland/ tidal marsh ecotone. Upriver, Clapper Rails, Marsh Wrens, and *Ammodramus* sparrows are attracted to the York's mesohaline/polyhaline marshes, where saltmarsh cordgrass (*Spartina alterniflora*), saltmeadow cordgrass (*S. patens*), saltgrass *(Distichlis spicata)*, sea-oxeye *(Borrichia frutescens)*, sea-lavender *(Limonium carolinianum)*, and dense patches of black needlerush *(Juncus roemerianus)* are segregated by their respective physiological tolerances.

Across the peninsula to the southeast the James River's mesohaline conditions off Kingsmill and Hog Island become oligohaline (0.5–5 ppt) as the tidal reach approaches the mouth of the Chickahominy River. The brackish marshes here and along the upper York River are populated by big cordgrass *(S. cynosuroides)*, salt marsh bulrush *(Scirpus robustus)*, bull-tongue arrowhead *(Sagittaria lancifolia)*, Olney threesquare *(Schoenoplectus americanus)*, and dotted smartweed *(Polygonum punctatum)*.

As the Chickahominy River courses inland its salinity transitions from oligohaline to tidal fresh water (0–0.5 ppt). Aquatic communities in this system include yellow pond lily *(Nuphar lutea)*, pickerelweed *(Pontederia cordata)*, wild rice *(Zizania aquatica)*, arrow arum *(Peltandra virginica)*, narrow-leafed *(Typha angustifolia)*, and broad-leafed cattail *(T. latifolia)*, water dock *(Rumex verticillatus)*, and tickseed sunflower *(Bidens coronata)*, circumstances favored by wintering waterfowl, nesting Least Bitterns, and an abundance of fall migrating Sora.

The riparian corridor along the James River from Jamestown northwest through the Chickahominy River is considered tidal hardwood swamp. An understory of winterberry *(Ilex verticillata)*, spice bush *(Lindera benzoin)*, possum-haw *(Viburnum nudum)*, sweetbay magnolia *(Magnolia virginiana)*, and swamp rose *(Rosa palustris)* compliments the bald cypress *(Taxodium distichum)*, black gum *(Nyssa sylvatica)*, and swamp tupelo *(N. biflora)* canopy. This community type is preferred breeding habitat for Ospreys, Bald Eagles, Great Blue Herons, Eastern Kingbirds, Northern Parulas, and Prothonotary and Yellow-throated warblers.

Palustrine communities such as those at the Greensprings Greenway, the interior of Jamestown Island, Longhill and Beaverdam swamps, and the heteroclite Grafton Ponds in lower York County (see **Birding Locations**) are scattered throughout the Colonial Historic Triangle. These ephemeral wetlands are variously dominated by swamp chestnut oak *(Quercus michauxii)*, willow oak *(Q. phellos)*, pin oak *(Q. palustris)*, white oak *(Q. alba)*, sweetgum *(Liquidambar styraciflua)*, and red maple *(Acer rubrum)*, with understory and shrub layers comprised of American hornbeam *(Carpinus caroliniana)*, American holly *(Ilex opaca)*, sweet pepper-bush *(Clethra alnifolia)*, sweetbay magnolia, and highbush blueberries *(Vaccinium spp.)*. Dead and dying trees in such wooded swamps are frequently occupied by Wood Ducks and Red-headed Woodpeckers. More importantly, these wetlands are critical for foraging Rusty Blackbirds during their winter residency here.

The rapid advancement of common reed *(Phragmites australis)* throughout Colonial Historic Triangle wetland communities has negatively impacted the ecological balance of these interdependent systems. As the plant spreads wetland vegetative diversity is reduced to a monoculture that offers minimal if any forage or shelter value to bird populations.

## Terrestrial Communities

The southern mixed hardwood forest once prevalent throughout the Colonial Historic Triangle is characterized by southern red oak *(Q. falcata)*, white oak, tulip poplar *(Liriodendron tulipifera)*, red maple, American beech *(Fagus grandifolia)*, sweetgum, hickory species *(Carya spp.)*, and loblolly pine *(Pinus taeda)*. Nesting Yellow-billed Cuckoos, Yellow-throated Vireos, and Summer and Scarlet Tanagers frequent its canopy layer. This forest type's understory of flowering dogwood *(Cornus florida)*, red bud *(Cercis canadensis)*, sassafras *(Sassafras albidum)*, black cherry *(Prunus serotina)*, American hornbeam, sourwood *(Oxydendrum arboreum)*, persimmon *(Diospyros virginiana)*, American holly, and paw-paw *(Asimina troloba)*, combined with its shrub layer of bayberry/wax myrtle *(Myrica spp)*, strawberry bush *(Euonymus americana)*, mountain laurel *(Kalmia latifolia)*, and deerberry/blueberry is occupied during the breeding season by Acadian Flycatchers, Blue-gray Gnatcatchers, Wood Thrushes, Ovenbirds, and Kentucky and Hooded warblers. Relatively mature examples of this diverse community may be experienced at Bassett Hall Woods, York River State Park, New Quarter Park, and the College of William and Mary woods (see **Birding Locations**).

Remnants of the area's rural agricultural heritage continue to be sustained in the northwest corner of the Colonial Historic Triangle. Scattered about this landscape are discontinuous plant communities, each with its respective avian correlates, that range from early-successional clear-cuts dominated by emergent mixtures of broom sedge *(Andropogon virginicus)*, bramble *(Rubus spp.)*, and eastern redcedar *(Juniperus virginiana)* to maturing loblolly pine, red maple, tulip poplar, and sweetgum aggregations. These continuously transitioning communities attract Northern Bobwhite, Prairie Warblers, Yellow-breasted Chats, Grasshopper Sparrows, Blue Grosbeaks, and Indigo Buntings.

Residential neighborhoods and commercial enterprises are (and increasingly will be) fact-of-life "habitats" across the region. The land use elements in these intensely manipulated developments function as strongholds for many of the locality's habitat generalists including, unfortunately, the pestilence of invasive non-native species. Nevertheless, their myriad botanically diverse landscapes, bird feeders, manicured golf links and water courses have proven to be oases for out-of-season hummingbird species, wintering Baltimore Orioles, flocks of eruptive winter finches, and those much anticipated seasonal rarities such as Eurasian Wigeon, White-winged Dove, Townsend's Solitaire, Black-headed Grosbeak, Painted Bunting, and Western Tanager.

*The very uprightness of the pines and maples asserts the ancient rectitude and vigor of nature. Our lives need the relief of such a background, where the pine flourishes and the jay still screams.*

Henry David Thoreau
from *A Week on the Concord and Merrimac Rivers*

# Ornithology in the Colonial Historic Triangle

*'If that unspeakably glorious spectacle is ornithology, then I am an ornithologist. I had no idea that such splendor existed. You must tell me much, much more.'*

Amos Jacob to Dr. Stephen Maturin
from *The Hundred Days* by Patrick O'Brian

The Colonial Historic Triangle became known to the birding community in 1946 through notes published by Raymond Beasley in the Virginia Society of Ornithology's journal *The Raven*. During the subsequent decade Fred Scott, Charles (Mo) Stevens and Dr. John Grey spent a great deal of time scouring local communities and waterways for birds, especially in lower York County. Scott and Grey posted many notes and articles about the region's avifauna in *The Raven*, as did state forester Charles Steirly, who described the diversity of bird populations in the Hog Island, Surry County, complex. Throughout the 1950s Dr. Grey, Martha Armstrong, Ed and Norma Katz, Bob McCartney, Charles Nimmo, and Dick Mahone, among others, birded local environs as an informal group known as the Hickory Neck Club. Unfortunately, little of the information gathered during their outings is extant.

The transition from birding to more protocol driven field ornithology found its way to Williamsburg in 1956 with the arrival of Dr. Mitchell Byrd at the College of William and Mary. Throughout the ensuing 6 decades Mitchell's tireless teaching, field work, banding activities, and mentoring, here and across the Commonwealth, redefined fundamental understandings of bird populations at the ecosystem level. Even as he guided students through his and their research his penchant for finding birds anywhere and everywhere was, and still is, always at play.

Mitchell and former graduate student Dr. Bryan Watts established in 1990 the nationally acclaimed Center for Conservation Biology (CCB) at the College of William and Mary. Its comprehensive, rigorously designed field studies carried out by staff and graduate students are the foundation for the Center's leadership in avian ecology research. Those investigations have proved invaluable for elevating understandings of bird populations throughout the mid-Atlantic region with extensions into the gulf states, Alaska, and Central and South America. Among its numerous on-going studies the CCB, now also affiliated with Virginia Commonwealth University, monitors Osprey, Bald Eagle, Peregrine Falcon, Whimbrel, Red Knot, Eastern Whip-poor-will, Chuck-will's-widow, and *Ammodramus* sparrow populations. Its work with Virginia's one remaining Red-cockaded Woodpecker population in Sussex County has skillfully delivered that species from the brink of extirpation from the Commonwealth.

Dr. Dan Cristol arrived to occupy the College of William and Mary's ornithology instructor aerie in 1996. His ebullient enthusiasm for avian studies has positively directed many university graduate and undergraduate students. Dan's passion for birds has become institutionalized in the public discourse through the bi-weekly "Birding" column he scribes for *The Virginia Gazette* newspaper. He and fellow College of William and Mary faculty member Dr. John Swaddle have facilitated numerous student investigations of local bird species, especially with Eastern Bluebirds.

## Bird Banding

Bird banding projects initiated in the mid-1960s by Mitchell Byrd and later by Charles Hacker at their respective York County home sites began to add substance to the limited anecdotal record of the Colonial Historic Triangle's songbird movements. In 1969 Mitchell and graduate student Bob Kennedy established a formalized spring banding study in an early-stage successional field at the Population Ecology Laboratory site off South Henry Street in the City of Williamsburg. With the exception of 1973 that project was sustained by Ruth Beck through the spring of 1982 and enabled her to investigate Yellow-breasted Chat nesting ecology. Coincidentally, a fall banding project was operated at the same location by Ruth in 1972, 1974, 1975, 1977, 1981, and 1982. From those long-term migration season studies data about the occurrence of expected, but more significantly, cryptic and rare species that passed through the Colonial Historic Triangle were verified for the permanent record, elevating them from conjecture to confirmed. Equally significant from those field years were the number of people who came to know and understand the area's birdlife through Ruth's tutelage. Then and for more than 40 years thereafter her effusive fervor for ornithology has inspired not only hosts of College of William and Mary students, but the greater ornithological community, contributions that reverberate through the present.

## Surry Nuclear Power Plant Study

During 1973 and 1974 Dr. Byrd was assisted by erstwhile graduate students Bill Akers, Jerry Via and Bill Williams to complete an extensive avian community

assessment of Hog Island Wildlife Management Area in Surry County as prepa-
ratory documentation for the construction of the Surry Nuclear Power Station
adjacent to Hog Island. Analysis of the January through October 1974 weekly
surveys and parallel breeding bird surveys chronicled the occurrence of 197
species on Hog Island. This documentation provided the first comprehensive
overview of the annual seasonal distribution of bird populations in at least one
unique segment of the Colonial Historic Triangle.

## The Christmas and Spring Bird Counts

The first "Williamsburg" Christmas Bird Count (CBC) made the record books
on December 22, 1946. Between 8:00 a.m. and 5:00 p.m. that day Raymond
Beasley tallied 607 birds of 36 species as he traversed 13 miles on foot between the
College of William and Mary campus and Jamestown. A Yorktown CBC was ac-
complished during the 1947–1954 count periods, overlapping with a 1953 and 1954
Toano CBC, and a 1952 and 1953 Surry CBC. The Surry CBC, which incorporated
the current Hog Island Wildlife Management area, was redesigned as the Hog
Island CBC for the 1954, 1955 and 1960 count seasons, and a "Jamestown" CBC
was completed on December 20, 1958.

In the spring of 1977 several members of what would become the Williamsburg
Bird Club later that fall loosely organized a one-day outing fondly referred to
at the time as the Thunderbird Count. Even though the data from that informal venture were lost to the ethers of conviviality, the effort, modeled after a
Christmas Bird Count protocol, set the stage for the Williamsburg Bird Club's
1977 CBC and for subsequent Spring Bird Counts.

The current Williamsburg Christmas Bird Count was initiated on December
18, 1977, three months after the formation of the Williamsburg Bird Club. The
geographic placement of the count circle, centered at the Colonial Williamsburg Information Center (37° 16' 45.37" N; 76° 41' 55.47" W), was designed to
encompass Hog Island Wildlife Management Area in Surry County and the
broadest possible spectrum of habitats in both the York River and James River
watersheds. Over its 35-year history the count has averaged 108 species. The cumulative species list, including those documented during the aforementioned
"Williamsburg," Yorktown, Jamestown, Toano, Surry, and Hog Island CBCs,
stands at 187, enriched by such notables as Greater White-fronted Goose,
Cackling Goose, Eurasian Wigeon, American White Pelican, American Avocet,
Short-eared Owl, Rufous Hummingbird, Ash-throated Flycatcher, White-eyed
Vireo, Lark Sparrow, and Western Tanager.

The Spring Bird Count has become as much of an annual event for the club as the
CBC. That one-day late April/early May Sunday event averages 153 species. A sum-

mary of the count's first seventeen years (1978-1994) was published in *The Raven* in 1994. Among the cumulative 242 species are Swallow-tailed Kite, Ruff, Red-necked Phalarope and Roseate Tern.

Data from both counts have contributed substantially to the delineation of the status and distribution of the Colonial Historic Triangle's resident and transient bird populations over time. Prime examples of this have been the population growth of Ospreys and Bald Eagles from the 1970s to the present, the arrival, dispersal, and subsequent local establishment of Mute Swans and House Finches, and the precipitous disappearance of Northern Bobwhite. The SBC's running totals trace the marked decline of Eastern Whip-poor-will, Chuck-will's–widow, Grasshopper Sparrow, and Seaside Sparrow, all of which were predictably easy to find through the count's first 2 decades. The CBC results speak volumes of the increased scarcity of Common Goldeneye and echo the disappearance of the Evening Grosbeak from local winter birdscapes.

## Avifauna of the Goodwin Islands and Taskinas Creek

A monitoring project to establish a seasonal distribution and breeding status baseline for avifauna on the Goodwin Islands in York County and at Taskinas Creek in York River State Park, James City County (see **Birding Locations**) was completed July 1991–June 1992 by the Chesapeake Bay National Estuarine Research Reserve System at the Virginia Institute of Marine Science. Specific habitat routes at each site were surveyed a minimum of 10 times during the year-long study. Results from those surveys, especially from the Goodwin Islands, provided information about birds that are infrequently detected in the Colonial Historic Triangle due to the limited observer access to the habitats these species frequent. Data from the Goodwin Islands confirmed that Virginia Rail, American Oystercatcher, Willet and Seaside Sparrow breed there and that Brant and Boat-tailed Grackles were present in larger numbers and for longer periods during the year than had been previously documented. Observations from the Taskinas Creek/York River State Park surveys shed some light on the breeding season incidence of Worm-eating Warbler, Black-and-white Warbler, and American Redstart in the park's mature upland forests.

## College Creek and the College Creek Hawk Watch

College Creek (see **Birding Locations**), with its visual sweep of the James River and access to a brackish water marsh, became a prime birding destination after the Colonial National Historic Parkway bridge was completed there in 1957. Observations gathered over many years at this location have documented more than 170 species, among the more exceptional of which are American White Pelican, Sandhill Crane, Black-headed Gull, Glaucous Gull, White-winged Dove, Lapland Longspur, and LeConte's Sparrow. Least Terns nested at the mouth of the creek from 1957 through 1966.

But it is the geographic positioning of this site that has proved to be the most ornithologically pertinent. The northeast projection of the Hog Island peninsula from the south side of the James River suggested it may serve as a leading line for north-bound migrating birds, especially vultures and diurnal birds of prey. Recognizing the potential of this for raptor migration study, Brian Taber in 1996 initiated what evolved into the College Creek Hawk Watch. Now a project of the Coastal Virginia Wildlife Observatory, the watch operates daily, weather permitting, from approximately 9:00 a.m. through 1:00 p.m. (EST) from mid-February through late May, making it the only vernal season effort of its kind in Virginia. Since its modest 1996 beginning (119 birds in 9½ hours) the site has logged 1,852 hours (average 109 hours/year) documenting the passage of 20,449 vultures and diurnal raptors. An average season chronicles 1,202 birds (11 birds/hour) with Turkey Vultures comprising 63% of the watch total, a mean of 762 per count year. In addition to the 2 vulture species, 15 diurnal raptor species including Swainson's Hawk, Northern Goshawk, and Golden Eagle have been recorded. The watch has shown that since 2000 Mississippi Kites have become rare but regular migrants through the Colonial Historic Triangle in May.

On those rare occasions during and/or after the passage of tropical cyclonic systems birders have found College Creek to be quite productive, the result of its position relative to the contours of the James River. Typically pelagic species such as Wilson's Storm-Petrel and Sooty and Bridled terns entrained by these storms get whisked by prevailing winds against the wooded shoreline inside the mouth of the creek and along the river's southeast to northwest channel. The two College Creek visitor parking lots, one fronting the river, the other fronting the marsh, offer excellent vantage points for scanning both the tidal marshland and the breadth of the estuary for errant birds.

## Greensprings Greenway Bird Surveys

The Greensprings Greenway in James City County (see **Birding Locations**) forms the centerpiece of a residential, recreational, agricultural, historically significant microcosm. More than 3,000 hours of regularly conducted bird surveys from November 1997 through February 2012 documented the occurrence of 217 species there, testament to the multipurpose trail system's habitat diversity. The presence of rare species (e.g. Eurasian Wigeon, Anhinga, Mississippi Kite, Olive-sided Flycatcher, Mourning Warbler, Clay-colored Sparrow, Lark Sparrow, and LeConte's Sparrow) notwithstanding, the greenway wetlands proved to be one of the most reliable places in the area to encounter foraging Rusty Blackbirds in winter and White Ibis in summer. Dead and dying trees throughout the same habitat were used by nesting Ospreys, Red-headed Woodpeckers, Tree Swallows, Brown-headed Nuthatches, and Prothonotary Warblers.

The long-term avifauna record from the greenway surveys spanned a period of significant natural and human induced change on and around the facility. In little more than a decade three neighborhoods surrounding the complex were built out, one of which permanently reduced adjacent farmland. Phase one of the Virginia Capital Trail (see **Birding Locations**) was routed over greenway wetlands and through both forested and cultivated lands. Simultaneously, native plant communities were negatively impacted by the proliferation of the white-tailed deer population and the rapid advancement of invasive species, particularly common reed and Japanese stilt grass *(Microstegium vimineum)*. A 1998 ice storm and hurricanes in 2003 and 2011 did considerable damage to the upland forest. Those cumulative alterations combined with the greenway's increased popularity and use encroached on and fragmented its once vibrant natural systems. Northern Bobwhite and Kentucky Warbler, both of which bred on the property in the late 1990s, disappeared entirely. Wood Thrushes and Ovenbirds, also breeders, were rarely encountered by 2011. Rock Pigeons, Northern Mockingbirds, and House Finches, on the other hand, appeared more regularly and in increasing numbers.

## New Quarter Park Bird Walks

Twice-a-month bird walks at New Quarter Park in York County (see **Birding Locations**) have been led by the Williamsburg Bird Club since June 2005. The collective effort from this public education endeavor has tracked the occurrence of 158 species at this multi-faceted public facility. The park's mature southern mixed hardwood forest supports breeding Red-headed Woodpeckers, Yellow-throated Vireos, Kentucky Warblers, and Summer and Scarlet tanagers. The birding groups often hear and sometimes see Clapper Rails along the marsh edges of Queens Creek. Yellow-crowned Night-Herons which breed nearby have proved to be rare and elusive there throughout the spring and summer months.

## Great Backyard Bird Count

Local participation in the annual Cornell Laboratory of Ornithology's Great Backyard Bird Count (GBBC) has grown dramatically since its 1998 inception. Williamsburg had 3 lists totaling 15 species for that first GBBC. By 2000 the local effort had grown to 100 checklists (tied for 6th in the state) reporting 88 species (also 6th in the state). The 2012 results had Williamsburg second highest in the state for both number of lists submitted with 281 and number of species reported with 108.

### The 2007 Virginia Society of Ornithology State Parks Breeding Bird Foray

Members of the Williamsburg Bird Club partnered with the newly organized Historic Rivers Chapter of the Virginia Master Naturalists to canvas as much of York River State Park (see **Birding Locations**) as possible for the June 2007 Virginia Society of Ornithology's State Parks Breeding Bird Foray. The team of 10 observers detected 67 species during 3 days of field work, the most intriguing of which were 3 highly territorial Black-and-white Warblers, a rare Colonial Historic Triangle breeder. Nesting Ospreys, Great Blue Herons, Great Crested Flycatchers, and Chipping Sparrows, plus recently fledged Bald Eagles were documented. Eastern Screech-Owls were tempted to return calls, yet no confirmed breeding evidence was found.

# The Williamsburg Bird Club

The Williamsburg Bird Club (http://www.williamsburgbirdclub.org/) fledged in September 1977 as the skillfully nurtured progeny of the venerable Hampton Roads Bird Club. Since then it has served the Colonial Historic Triangle's ornithological interests through a wide variety of educational endeavors and projects. The organization is officially sponsored by the College of William and Mary Biology Department, and as a result, has been afforded space in Millington Hall on the university campus to hold its September through May (except December) third-Wednesday-of-the-month meetings. As an affiliate of the Virginia Society of Ornithology the Williamsburg Bird Club hosted that organization's state-wide annual meetings in 1978, 1987, and 1995, the latter a joint conference with the Wilson Ornithological Society. The club's informative monthly newsletter, *The Flyer*, keeps members abreast of upcoming meetings and events, chronicles recent bird sightings, summarizes its monthly field trips and Christmas and spring bird counts, and serves as a forum for many enthralling anecdotes and stories crafted by its members. The organization ran a highly successful community-wide Bird Seed Savings Day from 1979 through 1991, enabling it to support Purple Martin and Eastern Bluebird nest box studies and to purchase a wealth of ornithological resources for the Williamsburg Regional Library. Annually the bird club awards two Bill Sheehan/Ruth Beck scholarships for College of William and Mary ornithology graduate students. More recently, the generosity of Bird Club members and Val and George Copping, proprietors of the local Wild Birds Unlimited, has enabled the club to present two scholarships for local elementary and middle school students to attend Nature Camp in Rockbridge County, Virginia.

# Past Presidents of the Williamsburg Bird Club

| | | | |
|---|---|---|---|
| 1977–1979 | Bill Williams | 1993–1995 | Ruth Beck |
| 1980–1981 | Ruth Beck | 1996–1997 | Lee Schuster |
| 1982 | Tom Armour | 1998–1999 | Joy Archer |
| 1983 | Thom Blair/Bob Cross | 2000 | Ruth Beck |
| 1984 | John Hertz | 2001–2002 | Hugh Beard |
| 1985 | Bill Snyder | 2003 | Ruth Beck |
| 1986–1988 | Bill Williams | 2004–2005 | Alex Minarik |
| 1989 | Ruth Beck | 2006–2007 | Bob Long |
| 1990–1991 | Tom Armour | 2008–2012 | Shirley Devan |
| 1992 | Dick Mahone | | |

# Ornithological Meetings in the Colonial Historic Triangle

**February 15–16, 1952**
The Virginia Society of Ornithology Nineteenth Annual meeting held at the College of William and Mary

**February 6–7, 1959**
The Virginia Society of Ornithology Annual meeting held at the College of William and Mary

**May 1–4, 1969**
The 50th Annual Meeting of the Wilson Ornithological Society, a joint conference with the Virginia Society of Ornithology-hosted by the College of William and Mary and the Hampton Roads Bird Club

**February 10–12, 1972**
North American Osprey Research Conference at the College of William and Mary

**May 19-21, 1978**
The Virginia Society of Ornithology Annual meeting held at the College of William and Mary, hosted by the Williamsburg Bird Club

**June 5–7, 1987**
The Virginia Society of Ornithology Annual meeting held at the College of William and Mary, hosted by the Williamsburg Bird Club

**May 4–7, 1995**
Joint conference of the Wilson Ornithological Society and the Virginia Society of Ornithology at the Fort Magruder Inn, hosted by the Williamsburg Bird Club

# Terms and Definitions

The terminology used in this document follows the conventions applied by Stephen C. Rottenborn and Edward S. Brinkley in *Virginia's Birdlife: An Annotated Checklist, Virginia Avifauna No. 7* published in 2007 by the Virginia Society of Ornithology.

## Relative Abundance

**Rare**: a species that is so scarce that it cannot be expected with any certainty, or one that occurs in a very specific and extremely limited habitat.

**Uncommon**: a species that occurs in small numbers or in limited habitat; such species are usually present within the proper season and habitat but may be difficult to find.

**Common**: a species that may be found most of the time in moderate numbers in the proper season and habitat.

**Abundant**: a species likely to be found in large numbers in the proper season and habitat.

**Local**: a species' distribution is sparse, typically the result of limited habitat.

**Irregular**: describes "species whose numbers show considerable interannual fluctuations."

## Status

**Transient**: describes species that pass through the Colonial Historic Triangle during normal migration.

**Visitor**: describes species that occur in Colonial Historic Triangle sporadically or irregularly, and often for short durations.

**Resident**: describes species that remain in the Colonial Historic Triangle for longer durations, either year-round or through either the breeding or winter season.

**Permanent resident**: describes species that "are present year-round," noting that turnover of individuals of these species "may occur due to the seasonal influx of birds breeding elsewhere and/or seasonal migration...during the nonbreeding season."

**Breeder**: a species for which there is direct evidence of nesting and/or raising young.

## Seasons

**Winter**: 1 December–28/29 February    **Summer**: 1 June–31 July
**Spring**: 1 March–31 May    **Fall**: 1 August–30 November

## Dates

Dates in the species accounts are the earliest and latest dates in the current local records. Where appropriate "extreme dates," arrival and/or departure dates beyond the historical average arrival, and/or departure dates for a species are annotated.

## Peak Counts

A peak count is "the highest number of individuals observed in a given location on a single day." Peak counts for those species that have been recorded on Christmas Bird Counts (CBC) and/or Spring Bird Counts (SBC) are given.

# Annotated Species Accounts

**Fulvous Whistling-Duck** *Dendrocygna bicolor*

There are six records for this rare visitor. Two birds at Queens Lake, *York* 30 Mar–12 Apr 1960 were part of the species' 1959 initial movement into Virginia. Subsequent records include one killed on Gordon Creek, Chickahominy River, *James City* Dec 1961; 10 "in Surry" 28 Apr 1979; and one at Queens Lake, *York* 6–9 Sep 1992.

**Peak Counts**: 42 at Hog Island, *Surry* 4–7 Nov 1961; 30 at Hog Island, *Surry* 1 Jan 1965.

**Greater White-fronted Goose** *Anser albifrons*

There are eight records for this rare, late fall transient and winter visitor 31 Oct– 8 Feb. Six of the records are from Hog Island, *Surry*; one from Little Creek Reservoir, *James City*; and, one near Chippokes Plantation State Park, *Surry*.

**Peak Count**: 4 at Hog Island, *Surry* 25–30 Nov 2006

**CBC**: 4 on 20 Dec 1981

**Snow Goose** *Chen caerulescens*

A rare and very local transient and winter visitor 4 Oct–13 Apr with extreme dates 24 Sep and 5 May. This species was recorded regularly at Hog Island, *Surry* through 1999.

**Peak Count**: 200+ at Hog Island, *Surry* 5 Feb 1987

**CBC**: 54 on 17 Dec 1991

**SBC**: one on 5 May 2002

The dark morph Snow Goose ("Blue Goose") is a rare and very local winter visitor.

**Peak Count**: 6 at Hog Island, *Surry* 28 Jan 1999

**Brant** *Branta bernicla*

There are twelve records for this rare transient and winter visitor; the most recent was one at Hog Island, *Surry* 22 Nov 2009.

**Peak Count**: 55 on the Goodwin Islands, *York* 11 Nov 1991

**Barnacle Goose** *Branta leucopsis*

There is one record. A single bird of unknown origin was at Drummond's Field, *James City* 25 Jan–13 Feb 1984.

## Cackling Goose *Branta hutchinsii*

There have been 2 records since the 2004 American Ornithologists' Union split; one was in Cheatham Pond, Cheatham Annex, *York* 18 Dec 2005; 2 were on Jamestown Island, *James City* 18 Mar 2011.

**CBC**: one on 18 Dec 2005

## Canada Goose *Branta canadensis*                                          **Breeder**

A common spring and fall transient and common permanent resident.

**Breeding:** incubating 21 Mar; downy young 5 May. The first evidence of local breeding was a nest at Hog Island, *Surry* in the summer of 1953. The next known breeding record was at Kingsmill, *James City* in March 1978.

**Peak Count:** 9,500 at Hog Island, *Surry* 17 Dec 1967.

**CBC**: 4,220 on the 2 Jan 1960 Hog Island, *Surry* CBC

**SBC**: 412 on 11 May 20

## Mute Swan *Cygnus olor*                                          **Breeder**

A rare permanent resident. The first record was one at Hog Island, *Surry* on the 17 Dec 1978 CBC. This species has been reported annually since 1984. The first evidence of breeding was at Cheatham Annex, *York* in 1989.

**Breeding**:  incubating 3 Mar; downy young 9 Apr

**Peak Count**: 10 in Kings Creek off Cheatham Annex, *York* 26 Feb 1993

**CBC**: 56 on 19 Dec 2004

**SBC**: 52 on 5 May 2005

Bill Williams

22

## Tundra Swan *Cygnus columbianus*

A common early spring and late fall transient and winter resident 27 Oct–5 Apr. There are two summer records: one at Camp Peary, *York* 1–5 Jun 1988; one at Gospel Spreading Farm, *James City* 1 Jul 2001.

**Peak Count**: 1,374 off College Creek, *James City* 11 Mar 2009

**CBC**: 317 on 17 Dec 1989

**SBC**: one on 3 counts: 28 Apr 1991; 29 Apr 2001; 30 Apr 2006

## Wood Duck *Aix sponsa*        **Breeder**

A common permanent resident and transient.

**Breeding**: small downy chicks 4 Apr–12 Jul

**Peak Count**: 150 at Jolly Pond, *James City* 18 Jul 1983

**CBC**: 23 on 18 Dec 1988

**SBC**: 131 on 7 May 1989

## Gadwall *Anas strepera*

An uncommon to common spring and fall transient and winter resident 13 Aug–22 Apr.

**Peak Count**: 50 on Camp Peary, *York* 13 Feb 1982.

**CBC**: 187 on 15 Dec 2002

**SBC**: 2 on 3 counts: 29 Apr 1984; 3 May 1987; 30 Apr 2006

## Eurasian Wigeon *Anas penelope*

There are eleven records, all but 2 of single males: Lake Powell, *James City* 15 Mar–11 Apr 1959; York River at the Naval Weapons Station, *York* 25–26 Feb 1970; Lake Powell, *James City* 14–31 Mar 1984; Hog Island, *Surry* 19 Nov 1988; Jolly Pond, *James City* 19–21 Mar 1994; Barlow's Pond, *James City/York* 20 Jan 1995; Greensprings Greenway Trail, *James City* 16 Mar 2003; Cheatham Lake, Cheatham Annex, *York* 18 Dec 2005; Powhatan Secondary, *James City* 21 Dec 2008–24 Feb 2009. A male and a gray morph female were at the Greensprings Greenway Trail 11 Oct and 14 Nov 2009.

**Peak Counts**: 2 at the Greensprings Greenway Trail, *James City* 11 Oct and 14 Nov 2009

**CBC**: one on 2 counts: 18 Dec 2005 and 21 Dec 2008

## American Wigeon *Anas americana*

An uncommon to common spring and fall (extreme early date 29 Aug) transient and winter resident 6 Oct–11 May.

**Peak Count**: 450 at Hog Island, *Surry* 17 Dec 1967

**CBC**: 289 on 17 Dec 1995

**SBC**: 2 on 28 Apr 1991

## American Black Duck *Anas rubripes*       **Breeder**

An uncommon spring and fall transient and winter resident, and rare summer resident.

**Breeding**: 14-egg nest 12 Apr 1983; 11-egg nest 29 Apr 1990

**Peak Count**: 1,260 at Hog Island, *Surry* 17 Dec 1967

**CBC**: 797 on 20 Dec 1981

**SBC**: 6 on 5 May 1985

## Mallard *Anas platyrhynchos*       **Breeder**

A common permanent resident and spring and fall transient.

**Breeding**: adult with downy young 24 May

**Peak Counts**: 2,000 at Hog Island, *Surry* on two dates: 19 Nov 1966 and 17 Dec 1967

**CBC**: 2,336 on 20 Dec 1981

**SBC**: 106 on 29 Apr 2012

A male Mallard × American Black Duck hybrid was at Drummond's Field, *James City* 13 Apr 2012

## Blue-winged Teal *Anas discors*       **Breeder**

A common fall transient 27 Jul–15 Nov. This species is a rare winter visitor and summer resident and an uncommon spring transient 15 Mar–20 May.

**Breeding**: 4 broods at Hog Island, *Surry* during the summer of 1953

**Peak Counts**: 28 at Drummond's Field, *James City* 10 Apr 1980; 100 at Hog Island, *Surry* 24 Aug 1989.

**CBC**: 8 on 18 Dec 1991

**SBC**: 18 on 29 Apr 2012

## Cinnamon Teal *Anas cyanoptera*

There is one record of 1–6 birds at Hog Island, *Surry* 14–17 Oct 1998.

## Northern Shoveler *Anas clypeata*        **Possible Breeder**

An uncommon transient and rare winter resident 4 Aug–1 May. This species is rare in summer.

**Breeding**: 3 very recently fledged young at Hog Island, *Surry* 10 Jul 1979 suggested breeding "nearby"

**Peak Count**: 200 at Hog Island, *Surry* 1 Mar 1996

**CBC**: 15 on 20 Dec 1987

**SBC**: 2 on 3 counts: 29 Apr 1984; 1 May 1988; 7 May 2000

## Northern Pintail *Anas acuta*

A formerly common to abundant late fall through spring transient and winter resident. This species is now uncommon to rare 2 Sep–16 Apr.

**Peak Count**: 15-20,000 at Hog Island, *Surry* 28 Jan 1981

**CBC**: 2,238 on 17 Dec 1978

## Green-winged Teal *Anas crecca*

A common transient and winter resident 4 Aug–11 May.

**Peak Count**: 1,000 at Hog Island, *Surry* 4 Mar 1990

**CBC**: 470 on 16 Dec 1990

**SBC**: 48 on 29 Apr 1990

Mike Millin

## Canvasback *Aythya valisineria*

Recorded all months, this species is a common transient and winter resident 10 Oct–15 Mar becoming rare by 1 Apr. One was at Cheatham Annex, *York* 29 Aug–12 Sep 1981.

**Peak Count**: 3,000 in the York River off Camp Peary, *York* 2 Dec 1995

**CBC**: 10,701 on 16 Dec 2001

**SBC**: 2 on 29 Apr 1990

### Redhead *Aythya americana*

A rare to uncommon transient and winter resident 27 Nov–24 Mar with extreme dates 10 Oct and 7 Apr.

**Peak Count**: 162 off Felgates Creek, *York* 3 Mar 2004

**CBC**: 300 on the 1 Jan 1954 *Surry* CBC

Bill Williams

### Ring-necked Duck *Aythya collaris*

A common transient and winter resident 24 Oct–15 Mar becoming rare by 1 Apr; extreme date 28 May.

**Peak Count**: 3,000 at Hog Island, *Surry* 6 Jan 1974

**CBC**: 1,539 on 16 Dec 2007

**SBC**: one on 9 May 1981 and 29 April 2012

### Greater Scaup *Aythya marila*

A rare transient and winter resident 27 Oct–25 Apr with an extreme date of 9 May.

**Peak Count**: 250 in the York River, *York* 5 Apr 1982

**CBC**: 9 on the 23 Dec 1952 Yorktown CBC

**SBC**: one on 11 May 1997

### Lesser Scaup *Aythya affinis*

A common transient and winter resident 10 Oct–15 May; extreme dates 2 Sep and 2 Jun.

**Peak Count**: 500 in the James River off Kingsmill, *James City* 5 Apr 1982

**CBC**: 501 on 16 Dec 2007

**SBC**: 31 on 6 May 1978

### Surf Scoter *Melanitta perspicillata*

A rare transient and winter visitor 14 Oct–19 Apr.

**Peak Count**: 21 at Yorktown, *York* 31 Jan 2004

**CBC**: 130 on the 23 Dec 1952 Yorktown CBC

## White-winged Scoter *Melanitta fusca*

A rare transient and winter visitor with twelve records 12 Nov–25 Apr.

**Peak Count**: 850 in the York River, *York* 2 Mar 1947

**CBC**: 250 on the 23 Dec 1952 Yorktown CBC

## Black Scoter *Melanitta americana*

A rare transient and winter visitor with eight records 29 Oct–25 Apr.

**Peak Count**: 4 in the York River near Yorktown, *York* 25 Apr 1990.

**CBC**: 184 on the 28 Dec 1951 Yorktown CBC

## Long-tailed Duck *Clangula hyemalis*

A rare transient and winter visitor 7 Nov–22 Mar.

**Peak Count**: 233 off the mouth of the York River, *York* 11 Feb 1953

**CBC**: 6 on 18 Dec 1977

## Bufflehead *Bucephala albeola*

A common transient and winter resident 15 Oct–12 Apr becoming uncommon to rare by late April with an extreme date of 9 May.

**Peak Counts**: 329 at Yorktown, *York* 23 Dec 1952; 250 at Hog Island, *Surry* 24 Jan 1997

**CBC**: 360 on 15 Dec 2002

**SBC**: 3 on 5 May 1978

## Common Goldeneye *Bucephala clangula*

A rare to uncommon transient and winter resident 4 Nov–27 Mar with three April records.

**Peak Count**: 1,100 off York River State Park, *James City* 11 Mar 1983

**CBC**: 328 on the 20 Dec 1950 Yorktown CBC

## Hooded Merganser *Lophodytes cucullatus*

A common transient and winter resident 23 Oct–15 Mar, becoming rare by 1 Apr with records as late as 30 May.

**Peak Count**: 300 at Hog Island, *Surry* 30 Nov 1989

**CBC**: 471 on 22 Dec 1996

**SBC**: 2 on 29 Apr 2007

### Common Merganser *Mergus merganser*

A rare transient and winter resident 6 Nov–30 Mar with an extreme date of 2 May.

**Peak Count**: 45–50 at Hog Island, *Surry* 13 Feb 1986

**CBC**: 200 on the 28 Dec 1951 Yorktown CBC

**SBC**: 3 on 2 May 1993

### Red-breasted Merganser *Mergus serrator*

A rare spring and fall transient and common winter resident 30 Oct–9 Jun with an extreme date of 22 Jun.

**Peak Count**: 500 in the James River off Kingsmill, *James City* 23 Mar 1981

**CBC**: 350 on 15 Dec 2002

**SBC**: 5 on 3 May 1992 and 2 May 1993

### Ruddy Duck *Oxyura jamaicensis*

A common to abundant transient and winter resident 26 Sep–16 May and rare summer visitor 2 Jun–9 Aug.

**Peak Count**: 15,000 at Yorktown, *York* 15 Jan 1981

**CBC**: 152,688 on 22 Dec 1996

**SBC**: 372 on 29 Apr 2007

### Northern Bobwhite *Colinus virginianus*       **Breeder**

This formerly uncommon to common species has declined dramatically since the 1990s and is now rare and very local, likely sustained by captive-released birds.

**Breeding**: downy young 25 Jul; a nest with eggs 24 Aug had downy young 29 Aug.

**Peak Counts**: 10–40 on a daily basis at Kingsmill, *James City* Sep–Oct 1980; 50 on Cheatham Annex, *York* 25 Jul 1982 and 7 May 1984

**CBC**: 102 on 16 Dec 1984

**SBC**: 130 on 15 May 1983

## Wild Turkey *Meleagris gallopavo* **Breeder**

A rare permanent resident.

**Breeding**: downy young by 27 May

**Peak Counts**: 30 on Cheatham Annex, *York* 27 Jan 1979; a 4 Jun 1980 Naval Weapons Station, Yorktown, *York* survey estimated the total population there was 200.

**CBC**: 27 on 14 Dec 2003

**SBC**: 17 on 11 May 1997

Fred Blystone

## Ring-necked Pheasant *Phasianus colchicus* **Former Breeder**

An introduced resident now extirpated with scattered reports of locally introduced individuals through Oct 2008. Of interest were 2 Black-necked Pheasants *P. c.* (unidentified subspecies) on the 2 Jan 1960 Hog Island CBC.

**Breeding**: adults with young 8 Jul

**Peak Count**: 50 at Cheatham Annex, *York* 30 Sep 1979

**CBC**: 27 on 16 Dec 1979

**SBC**: 28 on 4 May 1980

## Red-throated Loon *Gavia stellata*

An uncommon to rare transient and winter resident 23 Oct–15 May.

**Peak Counts**: 79 at the mouth of the York River, *York* 11 Feb 1953; 33 at Yorktown, *York* 28 Dec 2006

**CBC**: 5 on 19 Dec 2004

## Common Loon *Gavia immer*

An uncommon transient and winter resident 8 Sep–29 May. There are 4 summer records including a single bird at Kingsmill, *James City* 6–13 Jul 1981.

**Peak Counts**: 43 from the College Creek Hawk Watch, *James City* 13 Apr 2011

**CBC**: 27 on 20 Dec 1998

**SBC**: 9 on 5 May 1996

### Pied-billed Grebe *Podilymbus podiceps* **Breeder**

An uncommon transient (by 3 Sep) and winter resident and rare summer breeder.

**Breeding**: adult feeding 3 downy chicks at Hog Island, *Surry* 14 Jul 2002

**Peak Count**: 15 on Jones Mill Pond, *York* 1 Jan 1984

**CBC**: 61 on 21 Dec 1980

**SBC**: 5 on 5 May 1988

### Horned Grebe *Podiceps auritus*

An uncommon to common transient and winter resident 10 Oct–29 Apr with extreme dates 26 May and 22 Jun. This species is especially common on the York River, *York* where staging groups are much in evidence from mid-March through early April.

**Peak Counts**: 1,111 at the mouth of the York River, *York* 11 Feb 1953; 560 off Felgates Creek, *York* 28 Mar 1993

**CBC**: 429 on 1 Feb 1954 Yorktown CBC

**SBC**: 2 on 30 Apr 1995

### Red-necked Grebe *Podiceps grisegena*

A rare transient and winter visitor 17 Nov–11 Apr, most often on the York River, *York*.

**Peak Count**: 10 at Little Creek Reservoir, *James City* 24 & 25 Mar 1994

### Western/Clark's Grebe *Aechmophorus sp.*

There is one record, Virginia's first. One was at Felgates Creek, *York* 4 Dec 1963. This observation was made prior to the 1985 American Ornithologists' Union *A. clarkii/A. occidentalis* split. Because no detailed description and/or photo of this bird were recorded, a species designation could not subsequently be determined.

### Sooty Shearwater *Puffinus griseus*

There is one record of one off College Creek, *James City* post Tropical Storm Ernesto 2 Sep 2006.

### Wilson's Storm-Petrel *Oceanites oceanicus*

There are four records of which two were following the passage of tropical storms. This species is rare at the mouth of York River, *York* Jun–Jul.

**Peak Count**: 8 off Kingsmill, *James City* post Tropical Storm/Hurricane Bertha 13 Jul 1996

**White-faced Storm-Petrel** *Pelagodroma marina*
There is one record. One was off Kingsmill, *James City* post Hurricane Fran
6 Sep 1996.

**Wood Stork** *Mycteria americana*
There are seven records for this rare spring and fall transient and summer visitor. Two birds were at Hog Island, *Surry* 11–19 Jul 1985. The most recent record
was a single bird at Cub Dam Creek, New Quarter Park, *York* 19 Apr 2008.

**Peak Count**: 5 flying over the James River, *James City* 15 Nov 1960

**Magnificent Frigatebird** *Fregata magnificens*
There are two records each of single birds: one photographed at Kingsmill,
*James City* post Hurricane David 6 Sep 1979; one over the James River off Jame-
stown, *James City* 27 Jun 2006.

**Northern Gannet** *Morus bassanus*
A rare to uncommon late fall through early spring transient (13 Nov–8 Apr;
extreme date 26 May); more common in spring, with most records at or near
Yorktown, *York*.

**Peak Count**: 400-500 at Yorktown, *York* 10 Mar 2003

**CBC**: one on 21 Dec 2008

**Double-crested Cormorant** *Phalacrocorax auritus*
A common to abundant transient and resident.

**Peak Count**: 5,000 at Yorktown, *York* 11 Apr 1983

**CBC**: 1,719 on 18 Dec 2011

**SBC**: 375 on 30 Apr 2006

**Great Cormorant** *Phalacrocorax carbo*
A rare winter and spring visitor 15 Oct–8 May.

**Peak Count**: 4 in the James River off Kingsmill, *James City* 26 Nov 1980

**CBC**: one on 16 Dec 1984 and 17 Dec 1989

**SBC**: one on 8 May 1994

### Anhinga *Anhinga anhinga* **Breeder**

There are seven records: 2 flying over Kingswood, *James City* 24 Oct 1991; one at the Greensprings Greenway Trail, *James City* 19 Jun 1999; one at Harwood's Mill Reservoir, *York* 18 Apr 2010; one near the Warhill Sports Complex, *James City* 2 May 2010; one at Hardwood's Mill Reservoir, *York* 12 May 2011; 1 to 2 at Harwood's Mill Reservoir, *York* 6 Apr–25 May 2012

**Breeding**: a nesting pair, Virginia's first, at Harwood's Mill Reservoir, *York* 11 Jun 2009

### American White Pelican *Pelecanus erythrorhynchos*

A rare visitor recorded all months except June. First recorded 26 Nov 1981, this and most of the subsequent records have been from or near Hog Island, *Surry*. Additional records include one at Yorktown, *York* 1 Jan 1995 and 2 off Yorktown, *York* 3 Mar 1998.

**Peak Count**: 33 off College Creek, *James City* 13 Apr 2012

**CBC**: 2 on 20 Dec 1992

**SBC**: 22 on 29 Apr 2012

### Brown Pelican *Pelecanus occidentalis*

A rare to uncommon fall through spring resident and rare summer visitor. This species was first recorded locally off Yorktown, *York* Jun/Jul 1982.

**Peak Count**: 100+ off Jamestown, *James City* 24 Feb 2008

**CBC**: 26 on 16 Dec 2007

**SBC**: 44 on 29 Apr 2007

### American Bittern *Botaurus lentiginosus*

Rarely reported, this species likely occurs more frequently than the 21 records indicate. There is one March record, six April records, two for May, and one each for July and August. Fall and winter records include two for October, seven in December, and one for January.

**Peak Count**: 2 at Hog Island, *Surry* 11 Jan 2009

**CBC**: one on 5 counts: on the 2 Jan 1956 Hog Island CBC; 17 Dec 1991; 18 Dec 1994; 20 Dec 1998; 17 Dec 2006

**SBC**: one on 29 Apr 2007

### Least Bittern *Ixobrychus exilis* **Breeder**

A rare summer resident 1 May–27 Aug.

**Breeding**: adult feeding 2 chicks at Hog Island, *Surry* 14 Jul 2002

**Peak Count**: 6–7 near Jamestown Island, *James City* 2 Aug 1985

### Great Blue Heron *Ardea herodias* **Breeder**

A common permanent resident and uncommon transient. This species nests in small localized colonies of ~5–8 pairs with larger colonies on Jamestown Island, *James City*, along Queens Creek, *York*, and on Beaverdam Creek, *York*.

**Breeding**: nest building 13 Feb; incubating 6 Mar

**Peak Counts**: 470 nesting pairs at Beaverdam Creek, *York* May/Jun 1988; 200 at Hog Island, *Surry* 4 Mar 1990; 187 at Hog Island, *Surry* 7 Sep 2007

**CBC**: 428 on 20 Dec 1992

**SBC**: 326 on 7 May 1989

Seig Kopinitz

### Great Egret *Ardea alba* **Breeder**

An uncommon to common transient and summer resident and rare winter resident. This species reportedly bred in the Chickahominy River swamps, possibly in *James City*, in the early 1900s.

**Breeding**: occupied nests May/Jun near Beaverdam Creek, *York* 1983–2006; one nest on Jamestown Island, *James City* May/Jun 2006

**Peak Counts**: 242 at Hog Island, *Surry* 26 Aug 1995; 117 nesting pairs at Beaverdam Creek, *York* May/Jun 1997

**CBC**: 21 on 19 Dec 2004

**SBC**: 50 on 11 May 2003

**Snowy Egret** *Egretta thula*                                    **Former Breeder**

A rare transient and summer visitor 18 Mar–6 Nov. This species reportedly bred in the Chickahominy River swamps, possibly in *James City*, in the early 1900s.

**Peak Count**: 50 at Hog Island, *Surry* 4 Aug 1993; 50 at Camp Peary, *York* 1 Sep 1996

**SBC**: 8 on 2 May 1982

Bill Williams

**Little Blue Heron** *Egretta caerulea*                          **Former Breeder**

A rare spring and fall transient and summer visitor 2 Apr–27 Oct. There is one winter record of one at Kingsmill, *James City* 4 Dec 1982. This species reportedly bred "in the swamps and creeks near Jamestown" in the early 1900s.

**Peak Count**: 10 at Hog Island, *Surry* 19 Jul 1985

**SBC**: 2 on 7 May 1989

**Tricolored Heron** *Egretta tricolor*

A rare spring (8 Mar–23 May) and fall transient (11 Jul–17 Oct).

**Peak Count**: 15 at Hog Island, *Surry* 12 Aug 1996

## Cattle Egret *Bulbulcus ibis*

A rare spring (9 Mar–25 May; extreme date 16 Jun) and fall (23 Jul–29 Oct) transient.

**Peak Count**: 24 at Jamestown Island, *James City* 7 May 1980

**SBC**: 14 on 3 May 1992

Fred Blystone

## Green Heron *Butorides virescens*                     **Breeder**

A common transient and summer resident and rare winter visitor 25 Mar–17 Nov. One was at Seaford, *York* 29 Dec 1950.

**Breeding**: nest with young by 15 Jun; nest with eggs 2 Jul

**Peak Counts**: 12 at the Greensprings Greenway Trail, *James City* 23 Apr 2006; 15 at the Greensprings Greenway Trail, *James City* 6 Jul 2009 & 10 Jul 2011

**SBC**: 26 on 3 May 1987

**CBC**: one on several counts; most recently 17 Dec 2000

Bill Williams

### Black-crowned Night-Heron *Nyticorax nyticorax* **Former Breeder**

Recorded all months except February, this species is a rare transient (25 Mar–20 Nov) and a rare winter resident and summer visitor. It reportedly bred in the Chickahominy River swamps, possibly in *James City*, in the early 1900s.

**Peak Count:** 11 at Hog Island, *Surry* 9 Sep 1974

**CBC:** 5 on 17 Dec 1991

**SBC:** 9 on 7 May 1989

---

### Yellow-crowned Night-Heron *Nyctanassa violacea* **Breeder**

A rare and highly localized transient and summer resident 9 Mar–31 Oct; most often found at the Queens Creek marina at Queens Lake, *York* or at College Creek, *James City*.

Joe Piotrowski

**Breeding:** courtship display 5 Apr; incubating "early" May

**Peak Counts:** 4 adults at Queens Lake, *York* 5 Apr 1993; 4 juveniles at Queens Lake, *York* 7 Sep 2009; 3 juveniles at College Creek, *James City* 5 Sep 2009

**SBC:** 7 on 29 Apr 2007

---

### White Ibis *Eudocimus alba*

A rare late summer through early fall transient 3 Jul–2 Oct. This species was first reported locally from Queens Creek, *York* 24 Jul–4 Aug 1968.

**Peak Count:** 40-45 at Hog Island, *Surry* 7 Jul 1993

---

### Glossy Ibis *Plegadis falcinellus*

A rare spring (16 Mar–26 May) and mid-summer through fall (11 Jul–29 Nov) transient.

**Peak Count:** 36 flying over the College of William and Mary Population Ecology Lab site, Williamsburg 2 Apr 1990

**SBC:** 14 on 28 Apr 1991

**Black Vulture** *Coragyps atratus*                                    **Breeder**
An uncommon permanent resident and uncommon spring and fall transient.
Data from the College Creek Hawk Watch, *James City* indicate movements occur
9 Feb–26 May with a peak circa 15 Mar.

**Breeding**: downy young in nest 17 May

**Peak Counts**: 50 at the College Creek Hawk Watch, *James City* 11 Mar 2006;
64 at Settlers' Mill, *James City* 23 Nov 2008

**CBC**: 184 on 19 Dec 1982

**SBC**: 89 on 29 Apr 2012

---

**Turkey Vulture** *Cathartes aura*                                    **Breeder**
A common permanent resident and fall and spring transient. Data from the
College Creek Hawk Watch, *James City* indicate spring migration occurs
9 Feb–28 May with a peak circa 28 Mar.

**Breeding**: nest with 2 eggs 10 Apr 1985; nest with 2 downy young 19 May 1991

**Peak Counts**: 167 at the College Creek Hawk Watch, *James City* 20 Mar 2009.

**CBC**: 347 on 18 Dec 2011

**SBC**: 234 on 26 Apr 2009

---

**Osprey** *Pandion haliaetus*                                    **Breeder**
A common spring and fall transient and summer resident (14 Feb–28 Nov),
and rare winter visitor. Data from the College Creek Hawk Watch, *James City*
data indicate spring migration occurs 14 Feb–24 May with a peak circa 18 Apr.

**Breeding**: incubating by 8 Mar

**Peak Counts**: 28 active nests on Bay Tree Neck, *York* 6 May 1934; 52 at the College
Creek Hawk Watch, *James City* 18 Apr 2007

**CBC**: 3 on 19 Dec 1993; 1–2 have been recorded on 6 of the last 8 CBCs

**SBC**: 178 on 1 May 2011

---

**Swallow-tailed Kite** *Elanoides forficatus*
There are two records, both of single birds: an adult at Riverview Plantation,
*James City* 3 May 1987; an immature at Hog Island, *Surry* flew into *James City*
over College Creek 28 Aug 1991.

---

**White-tailed Kite** *Elanus leucurus*
There is one record, Virginia's first. One was at Tomahund Plantation, *Charles
City* 0.9 miles west of the Chickahominy River 5 Jun 1988.

### Mississippi Kite *Ictinia mississippiensis*

A rare spring transient 9 Apr–2 Jun. One was at College Creek, *James City* post Tropical Storm Dennis 5 Sep 1999. This species was first recorded at Hog Island, *Surry* 11 May 1997. Twenty-four of the 29 individuals recorded have been within the 2–27 May period, all at the College Creek Hawk Watch, *James City*.

**Peak Count**: 9 over the Williamsburg-Jamestown Airport, *James City* 12 May 2007

**SBC**: one at Hog Island, Surry 11 May 1997

### Bald Eagle *Haliaeetus leucocephalus*             **Breeder**

A formerly rare now common permanent resident, transient, and summer and winter visitor. Data from the College Creek Hawk Watch, *James City* indicate spring migration occurs 22 Feb–24 May, with a peak circa 21 May.

**Breeding**: A 1962 survey found 14 nests, 12 in *James City*, 2 in *York*. No pairs nested in either jurisdiction in 1977. The 2011 survey found 49 active nests: 32 in *James City*, 13 in *York*, and 4 on Hog Island, *Surry*. Incubation may commence by late December with mid-to late February more typical.

**Peak Counts**: 23 at Hog Island, *Surry* 9 Aug 2007; 34 at the College Creek Hawk Watch, *James City* 19 May 2010

**CBC**: 58 on 20 Dec 2009

**SBC**: 76 on 11 May 2003

Bill Williams

## Northern Harrier *Circus cyaneus*

An uncommon transient and winter resident 1 Aug–25 May. There are two summer records, both of single birds at York River State Park, *James City* 5 Jul 1978 and 10 Jun 1979, respectively. Data from the College Creek Hawk Watch, *James City* indicate spring migration occurs 10 Feb–10 May with a peak circa 22 Apr.

**Peak Count**: 12 on 3 Apr 2011 included 10 at the College Creek Hawk Watch, *James City* plus 2 at the Greensprings Greenway Trail, *James City*

**CBC**: 8 on 17 Dec 1989

**SBC**: 9 on 2 May 1993

## Sharp-shinned Hawk *Accipiter striatus*      **Probable Breeder**

An uncommon spring (19 Feb–17 May) and fall (16 Aug–21 Nov) transient and winter resident. Data from the College Creek Hawk Watch, *James City* indicate spring migration occurs 8 Feb–22 May with a peak circa 22 Apr.

**Breeding**: reports throughout the summer months suggest local breeding.

**Peak Count**: 38 at the College Creek Hawk Watch, *James City* 5 May 1999

**CBC**: 13 on 19 Dec 1982

**SBC**: 8 on 3 May 1992

## Cooper's Hawk *Accipiter cooperii*      **Breeder**

An uncommon transient and rare permanent resident. College Creek Hawk Watch, *James City* data indicate spring migration occurs 28 Feb-26 May with a peak circa 21 Apr.

**Breeding**: nesting pair on the College of William and Mary campus, Williamsburg with 4 large nestlings 17 Jun 2010

**Peak Count**: 9 at the College Creek Hawk Watch, *James City* 11 Mar 2010

**CBC**: 5 on 19 Dec 2004

**SBC**: 4 on 1 May 2005

## Northern Goshawk *Accipiter gentilis*

A rare transient and winter visitor with five records 20 Dec–24 Apr. A hatch-year bird was seen by many observers at Hog Island, *Surry* 13 Jan–13 Feb 1984.

### Red-shouldered Hawk *Buteo lineatus* **Breeder**

An uncommon permanent resident and spring transient. College Creek Hawk Watch, *James City* data indicate spring migration occurs 27 Feb–21 Apr with a peak circa 15 Apr.

**Breeding**: carrying nesting material 10 Mar; incubating by 22 Mar

**Peak Count**: "In the wooded sections surrounding Williamsburg, Va…22 sets of eggs were collected from March 15th to April 18th, 1935".*

**CBC**: 23 on 19 Dec 2010

**SBC**: 17 on 29 Apr 2012

*Unpublished field notes of F. M. Jones

### Broad-winged Hawk *Buteo platyperus*

A rare spring (2 Apr–6 June) and fall (7 Sep–14 Oct) transient and rare summer visitor. Data from the College Creek Hawk Watch, *James City* indicate spring migration occurs 10 Apr–23 May with a peak circa 30 Apr. An injured adult male was recovered off Penniman Road, *York/James City* 16 Dec 1982.

**Peak Count**: 15 flying over News Road, *James City* 27 Apr 1984

**SBC**: 9 on 11 May 2003

### Swainson's Hawk *Buteo swainsoni*

There are two records, both of single birds: one at Kingsmill, *James City* 2 Sep 1982; one at the College Creek Hawk Watch, *James City* 22 Apr 2001.

### Red-tailed Hawk *Buteo jamaicensis* **Breeder**

An uncommon permanent resident and spring and fall transient. Data from the College Creek Hawk Watch, *James City* indicate spring migration occurs 20 Feb–24 May with a peak circa 21 Apr.

**Breeding**: incubating 31 Mar; feeding young in nest 5 May

**Peak Count**: 9 at the College Creek Hawk Watch, *James City* 20 Feb 2004

**CBC**: 34 on 17 Dec 1978

**SBC**: 23 on 5 May 1996 and 1 May 2011

### Rough-legged Hawk *Buteo lagopus*

A rare transient and winter visitor with nine records 8 Nov–31 Mar. A dark morph bird was at Hog Island, *Surry* 5–21 Feb 1982.

**Peak Count**: 2 near Yorktown, *York* 2 Jan 1954; 2 at Camp Peary, *York* 9 Feb 1997

**CBC**: 2 on the 1 Feb 1954 Yorktown CBC

**Golden Eagle** *Aquila chrysaetos*
A rare fall through spring transient 28 Oct–29 Apr with seven to eight records, all of single birds.

**Yellow Rail** *Coturnicops noveboracensis*
There is one confirmed record. One was found dead at Cheatham Annex, *York* 11 Oct 1980.

**Black Rail** *Laterallus jamaicensis*
There is one record. One was reported near Seaford, *York* 21 Aug 1949.

**Clapper Rail** *Rallus longirostris*
**Breeder**
An uncommon permanent resident and fall and spring transient.

**Breeding**: nest with eggs 6 May; nest with 1 young 3 Jun; young in nest 5 Jun

**Peak Count**: 13 at Bay Tree Beach Road, Seaford, *York* 19 Nov 2011

**CBC**: 21 on 20 Dec 1998

**SBC**: 28 on 8 May 1994

**King Rail** *Rallus elegans*
**Breeder**
An uncommon permanent resident and fall and spring transient; likely more numerous than records indicate, made problematic by the difficulty of separating this species from Clapper Rail by voice.

**Breeding**: nest with 8 eggs at Hog Island, *Surry* 5 Jun 1952; nest with 7 eggs at Hog Island, *Surry* 3 Jul 1960

**Peak Count**: 5-6 at College Creek, *James City* 6 Oct 1995

**CBC**: 3 on the 1 Jan 1954 Toano CBC

**SBC**: 2 on 3 May 1998

**Virginia Rail** *Rallus limicula*
**Breeder**
A rare transient, winter resident, and summer breeder; no August records.

**Breeding**: young in nest 7 Jun

**Peak Count**: 6 on Jamestown Island, *James City* 26 Feb 1991

**CBC**: 7 on 16 Dec 1984

**SBC**: 2 on 3 May 1998

**Sora** *Porzana carolina*

A common to abundant fall transient 26 Aug–26 Nov, especially in the Chicka-hominy River marshes, *James City*. This species is rare in winter and a rare spring transient.

**Peak Count**: 2,000+ in the Chickahominy River marshes off Shield's Point, *James City* after Tropical Storm Dean 30 Sep 1983

**CBC**: 10 on the 1 Jan 1954 Toano CBC

**SBC**: 3 on 3 May 1992

**Purple Gallinule** *Porphyrio martinica*

There are 4 records, all of single birds within the 16 Apr–23 May time period: near Norge, *James City* 29 Apr–10 May 1953; at Lake Powell, *James City* 5 May 1963; at Tutter's Neck Pond, Williamsburg 16 Apr 1967; at the Gospel Spreading Farm, *James City* 9–23 May 2004.

**Common Gallinule** *Gallinula galeata*

A rare spring (3 Apr–18 Jun) and fall (11 Sep–16 Oct) transient, with sixteen records, all of single birds. This species is probably more prevalent than current records indicate.

**CBC**: one on 20 Dec 1992

**American Coot** *Fulica americana*

An uncommon spring and fall transient and winter visitor (22 Oct–21 May) and rare summer resident.

**Peak Count**: 250–300 on Gordon Creek, Chickahominy River, *James City* 9 Dec 1979

**CBC**: 152 on 17 Dec 1978

**SBC**: 266 on 29 Apr 2007

**Sandhill Crane** *Grus canadensis*

There are four records, all from College Creek, *James City*: 2 on 10 May 2006; one on 20 May 2008; 2 over Hog Island, *Surry* 26 Apr 2011; one over Hog Island, *Surry* 24 May 2011

**Black-bellied Plover** *Pluvialis squatarola*

A rare spring (24 Mar–28 May) and fall (6 Aug–7 Dec) transient and rare winter visitor.

**Peak Count**: 25 at Hog Island, *Surry* 27 Oct 1982

**CBC**: 3 on 20 Dec 1950

**SBC**: 16 on 4 May 1986

### American Golden-Plover *Pluvialis dominica*
A rare and very irregular spring (4–22 Apr) and fall (22 Aug–29 Oct) transient.

**Peak Count**: 21 at Hog Island, *Surry* 15 Sep 1996

### Wilson's Plover *Charadrius wilsonia*
There are two records possibly of the same bird(s) at Hog Island, *Surry*; one to 2 on 10 & 11 Aug then 23 & 26 Sep 1987.

### Semipalmated Plover *Charadrius semipalmatus*
An uncommon spring and fall transient and summer visitor 28 Apr–18 Oct. Extreme fall dates include one at Seaford, *York* 25 Nov 1949 and 2 at Felgates Creek, *York* 22 Nov 2008. The single winter record was on the 19 Dec 2010 CBC.

**Peak Count**: 300 at Hog Island, *Surry* 6 Aug 1993

**CBC**: one on 19 Dec 2010

**SBC**: 112 on 11 May 1997

### Piping Plover *Charadrius melodus*
A rare visitor with five to six records. This species was documented annually (1949–1953) in winter at Seaford, *York* 25 Nov–8 Mar. All of these records, except one, were of single birds. There are 2 records of single birds at Hog Island, *Surry* 18 Jul 1994 and 7 & 11 May 1997.

**Peak Count**: 3 at Seaford, *York* 10 Feb–8 Mar 1952 (possibly 1951)

### Killdeer *Charadrius vociferus*                    **Breeder**
An uncommon to common local resident and transient.

**Breeding**: 2 nests with 4 eggs each 17 Mar; nest with eggs as late as 29 July

**Peak Count**: 80 at Drummond's Field, *James City* 29 Dec 1994

**CBC**: 125 on the 1 Feb 1954 Yorktown CBC

**SBC**: 46 on 29 Apr 2001

Brian Taber

**American Oystercatcher** *Haematopus palliatus* **Breeder**

There are six records for this rare spring and fall transient and rare summer resident near the mouth of the York River, *York*.

**Breeding**: territorial pairs on the Goodwin Islands, *York* Jun 2003 & 2008

**Peak Count**: 16; includes 12 on the Goodwin Islands, *York* plus 4 on Crab Neck, Seaford, *York* 10 May 2011.

**Black-necked Stilt** *Himantopus mexicanus*

A rare spring and fall transient with five records 18 Apr–5 May. There is one fall record.

**Peak Count**: 13 at Hog Island, *Surry* 22 Nov 1969

**American Avocet** *Recurvirostra americana*

A rare summer visitor and rare fall (8 Jul–19 Dec) and early spring (1–3 Mar) transient.

**Peak Count**: 29 at Hog Island, *Surry* 20 Nov 1983

**CBC**: one on 19 Dec 1993

**Spotted Sandpiper** *Actitis macularia*

An uncommon spring (26 Mar–2 Jun) and fall (4 Jul–8 Nov) transient and rare winter visitor to 12 Feb.

**Peak Count**: 13 at Hog Island, *Surry* 19 May 1974

**SBC**: 61 on 4 May 1980

**CBC**: one on 18 Dec 1977; 17 Dec 1978

**Solitary Sandpiper** *Tringa solitaria*

An uncommon spring (2 Apr–22 May) and fall (20 Jul–14 Oct) transient.

**Peak Count**: 8 on several May dates

**SBC**: 65 on 4 May 1986

**Greater Yellowlegs** *Tringa melanoleuca*

A common spring (21 Mar–12 Jun) and fall transient (15 Jul–10 Nov) and rare to uncommon winter resident.

**Peak Count**: 175 at Hog Island, *Surry* 11 May 1990

**SBC**: 66 on 6 May 1978

**CBC**: 34 on 20 Dec 1992

**Willet** *Tringa semipalmata* **Breeder**

A rare spring (26 Apr–3 Jun) and fall (1 Sep) transient and rare summer resident at the mouth of the York River, *York*.

**Breeding**: nest with downy young 23 May

**Peak Count**: 30 on the Goodwin Islands, *York* 15 Jun 1992

**SBC**: 3 on 30 Apr 1995

---

**Lesser Yellowlegs** *Tringa flavipes*

A common spring (17 Mar–22 May) and fall transient (16 Jul–25 Nov) and rare winter resident.

**Peak Counts**: 200 at Hog Island, *Surry* 16 Apr 1997; 75 at Hog Island, *Surry* 26 Aug 1998

**SBC**: 204 on 11 May 1997

**CBC**: 11 on 16 Dec 1979

---

**Upland Sandpiper** *Bartramia longicauda*

A rare spring (10 Apr–19 May) and fall (6–28 Aug) transient.

**Peak Count**: 4 at Hog Island, *Surry* 27 Aug 2004

---

**Whimbrel** *Numenius phaeopus*

A rare spring (8–25 May) and early fall (4 Aug–23 Sep) transient and rare winter visitor. The thirteen records include a single bird at Halfway Creek off the Colonial Parkway, *James City* 5 Jan 1971 and one at Hog Island, *Surry* 28 Oct 2007.

**Peak Count**: 45 near Blackstump Creek, Chickahominy River, *James City* 25 May 1985

---

**Hudsonian Godwit** *Limosa haemastica*

There are four fall (18 Aug–31 Oct) records and one spring record, all of single birds at Hog Island, *Surry*.

**SBC**: one photographed on 2 May 2010

---

**Marbled Godwit** *Limosa fedoa*

A rare spring (15 Mar–19 Apr) and fall (13 Jul–27 Sep) transient. Nine of the ten records are from Hog Island, *Surry*.

**Peak Count**: 2 at Hog Island, *Surry* 2–27 Sep 2007

### Ruddy Turnstone *Arenaria interpres*

There are twelve records for this rare spring (7–25 May) and fall (21 Jul–30 Aug) transient, with an extreme date of 10 Oct. This species is a rare winter visitor.

**Peak Count**: 5 near Yorktown, *York* 25 May 1981

**CBC**: one on 19 Dec 2004

### Red Knot *Calidris canutus*

There are three records: 15 at Seaford, *York* 21 Jan 1951; one at Kingsmill, *James City* 25 Apr 1983; 18 on the Goodwin Islands, *York* 20 May 1997.

### Sanderling *Calidris alba*

A rare to uncommon spring (10–22 May) and fall (22 Jul–11 Nov) transient and rare winter visitor.

**Peak Count**: 28 at Hog Island, *Surry* 19 May 1974

**CBC**: 150 on the 1 Feb 1954 Yorktown CBC

**SBC**: 9 on 11 May 2003

### Semipalmated Sandpiper *Calidris pusilla*

A common spring (14 Apr–11 Jun) and fall (15 Jul–11 Nov) transient.

**Peak Count**: 2,500 at Hog Island, *Surry* 6 Aug 1993

**SBC**: 66 on 11 May 1997

### Western Sandpiper *Calidris mauri*

A common to uncommon fall (3 Jul–25 Nov) transient and rare winter visitor.

**Peak Count**: 500 at Hog Island, *Surry* 25 Aug 1987

**CBC**: 22 on 20 December 1998

### Least Sandpiper *Calidris minutilla*

A common spring (20 Mar–4 Jun; extreme date 22 Jun) and fall (14 Jul–18 Oct) transient and rare winter visitor. There are no November or January records for this species.

**Peak Count**: 75 at Hog Island, *Surry* 11 Aug 1987

**CBC**: 14 on 21 Dec 1986

**SBC**: 175 on 5 May 1985

### White-rumped Sandpiper *Calidris fuscicollis*

A rare spring (29 Apr–11 Jun) and fall (18 Jul–23 Oct) transient.

**Peak Count**: 21 at Hog Island, *Surry* 20 Sep 1987

**SBC**: 4 on 6 May 1979 and on 2 May 2010

**Baird's Sandpiper** *Calidris bairdii*
There is one record of a single bird at Hog Island, *Surry* 19 Aug 1989.

**Pectoral Sandpiper** *Calidris melanotos*
An uncommon spring (15 Mar–14 May) and fall (18 Jul–17 Nov) transient.

**Peak Count**: 125 at Hog Island, *Surry* 1 Apr 1986

**SBC**: 25 on 6 May 1978

**Dunlin** *Calidris alpina*
An uncommon spring (28 Mar–3 Jun) and fall (8 Jul–30 Nov) transient and rare winter visitor. There is one July record and no August records.

**Peak Counts**: 309 at Hog Island, *Surry* 26 Oct 1974; 125 at Cheatham Annex, *York* 15 Feb 2008; 93 on the Goodwin Islands, *York* 10 May 2011

**CBC**: 37 on both the 21 Jan 1950 Yorktown CBC and the 20 Dec 1950 Yorktown CBC.

**SBC**: 29 on 11 May 1997

**Stilt Sandpiper** *Calidris himantopus*
A rare spring (13 Apr–11 May) and fall (20 Jul–11 Nov) transient.

**Peak Count**: 129 at Hog Island, *Surry* 25 Jul 1981

**SBC**: 3 on 5 May 1996

**Buff-Breasted Sandpiper** *Tryngites subruficollis*
A rare fall transient 14 Aug–25 Oct.

**Peak Count**: 13 at Hog Island, *Surry* 30 Aug 2010

**Ruff** *Philomachus pugnax*
There is one record of a single bird at Hog Island, *Surry* 4–7 May 1986.

**Short-billed Dowitcher** *Limnodromus griseus*
A rare to uncommon spring (1 Apr–16 May) and fall (8 Jul–23 Oct) transient and rare winter visitor.

**Peak Count**: 145 at Hog Island, *Surry* 27 Aug 1988

**CBC**: 11 on 17 Dec 1995

**SBC**: 177 on 11 May 1997

**Long-billed Dowitcher** *Limnodromus scolopaceus*
There are five fall (21 Jul–17 Oct) records, four of those from Hog Island, *Surry*.

**Peak Counts**: 2 at Hog Island, *Surry* 17 Oct 1982; 2 on the Goodwin Islands, *York* 9 Sep 1991; 2 at Hog Island, *Surry* 21 Jul 1996

## Wilson's Snipe *Gallinago delicata*

A common spring (~1 Mar–11 May) and fall (extreme date 19 Aug) transient and uncommon winter resident. There are numerous reports of >30 birds on March and November dates.

**Peak Count**: 100 at Drummond's Field, *James City* 21 March 1994

**CBC**: 43 on 20 December 2009

**SBC**: 15 on 29 April 1984

## American Woodcock *Scolopax minor*                    **Breeder**

A rare transient and resident, recorded all months.

**Breeding**: eggs in nest 24 Feb–20 Mar; hatched eggs 1 Apr; 4 hatched eggs 12 Apr

**Peak Count**: 8 at Archer's Hope, Colonial Parkway, *James City* 6 March 1996

**CBC**: 14 on 16 Dec 1979

**SBC**: 5 on 2 counts: 7 May 1989 and 30 Apr 1995

## Wilson's Phalarope *Phalaropus tricolor*

A rare spring (29 Apr–10 May) and fall (18 Jul–22 Sep) transient.

**Peak Count**: 11 at Hog Island, *Surry* 2 Sep 1974

**SBC**: one on 29 Apr 1990

## Red-necked Phalarope *Phalaropus lobatus*

A rare fall (21 Aug–11 Sep) and spring transient.

**Peak Counts**: 2 at College Creek, *James City* post Tropical Storm Dennis 5 Sep 1999; 2 at Hog Island, *Surry* 9 Sep 2007

**SBC**: one on 6 May 1978

## Red Phalarope *Phalaropus fulicarius*

There are two records, both of single birds at Hog Island, *Surry*: 4 Apr 1960 and 21-22 Oct 1983.

## Bonaparte's Gull *Chroicocephalus philadelphia*

A uncommon spring (to 24 May) and fall (from 27 Oct) transient and winter resident and rare summer visitor; peak numbers occur March through April.

**Peak Counts**: 600 off Felgates Creek, York River, *York* 6 Apr 1984; 565 from the Hog Island, *Surry* area 12 Mar 2008

**CBC**: 145 on 17 Dec 1991

**SBC**: 62 on 29 Apr 2012

**Black-headed Gull** *Chroicocephalus ridibundus*

There is one record. An adult was at College Creek, *James City* 14 Mar 1993.

**Little Gull** *Hydrocoloeus minutus*

There are three records, all from the James River, *James City*: one off Kingsmill 23 Mar 1985; 2–3 near Jamestown 23 Mar 1986; one from the Jamestown Ferry 6 Apr 1986.

**Laughing Gull** *Leucophaeus atricilla*

A common to abundant spring and fall transient and summer resident, and rare winter visitor. The typical spring arrival is ~15 Mar with a 25 Feb extreme date.

**Peak Count**: 1,050 along the James River, *James City* post Tropical Storm Fran 6 Sep 1996

**CBC**: 316 on 17 Dec 1991

**SBC**: 3,400 on 2 May 1993

**Franklin's Gull** *Leucophaeus pipixcan*

There are four records, all of single birds: at Queens Creek, *York* 12 May 1991; from the Jamestown Ferry, *James City* 11 Jun 1996; from the Jamestown Ferry, *James City* 4 Oct 1996; from the Jamestown Ferry, *James City* 12–15 Jun 2009.

**Ring-billed Gull** *Larus delawarensis*

An abundant transient and winter resident (19 Aug–21 May) and rare summer resident.

A wing-tagged individual observed at Cheatham Annex, *York* 15 Mar 1980 had been banded on Lake Huron in May/June 1975.

**Peak Count**: 5,000 in fields near Hog Island, *Surry* 8 Dec 1993

**CBC**: 2,973 on 18 Dec 1977

**SBC**: 1,202 on 2 May 1982

**Herring Gull** *Larus argentatus*

A common transient (21 Oct–15 May) and winter resident and uncommon summer resident.

**Peak Count**: 150 at Hog Island, *Surry* 10 Mar 1974

**CBC**: 490 on 17 Dec 1978

**SBC**: 258 on 6 May 1979

### Iceland Gull *Larus glaucoides*

There are four records, all of single first-cycle birds on the James River, from Kingsmill to the Jamestown/Scotland ferry wharf, *James City/Surry*: 17 January 1992; 1 Feb 1994; 25 Mar 1982; 19–22 Apr 1983.

Current consensus suggests all mid-Atlantic Iceland Gulls are *L. g. kumlieni.*

### Lesser Black-backed Gull *Larus fuscus*

A rare fall through spring visitor 19 Oct–7 May. This species was first recorded locally at Felgates Creek, *York* 20 Dec 1987. It has been recorded annually since 1991. Most of the recent observations have been on the James River, from Kingsmill and College Creek to the Jamestown/Scotland ferry wharf, *James City/Surry*.

**Peak Count**: 3 at College Creek, *James City* 17 Mar 2001 and 9 and 15 Feb 2006.

**CBC**: 2 on 20 Dec 1987 and 17 Dec 2006

**SBC**: one on 2 counts:  29 Apr 2007 and 4 May 2008

### Glaucous Gull *Larus hyperboreus*

There are seven records all of single first-cycle birds in winter (12 Jan–9 Mar). One lingered at College Creek, *James City* 24 Jan–6 Feb 1980. The most recent record was one at College Creek 28 Feb 2011.

### Great Black-backed Gull *Larus marinus*

An uncommon transient and winter resident and rare summer visitor.

**Peak Count**: 200 at Yorktown, *York* 15 Aug 1990

**CBC**: 121 on 17 Dec 1995

**SBC**: 49 on 16 May 1999

### Sooty Tern *Onychoprion fuscatus*

There are four records totaling some 33 individuals: 5 (1 deceased) at the Williamsburg-Jamestown Airport, *James City* post Hurricane David 6 Sep 1979; 3 off Kingsmill, *James City* post Hurricane Bertha 13 Jul 1996; 11 off Kingsmill, *James City* post Tropical Storm Fran 6 Sep 1996; 14 from College Creek, *James City* post Tropical Storm Ernesto 2 Sep 2006.

### Bridled Tern *Onychoprion anaethetus*

There are two records: one was off College Creek, *James City* 6 Sep 1996 post Tropical Storm Fran; 7 from College Creek, *James City* post Tropical Storm Ernesto 2 Sep 2006.

**Least Tern** *Sternula antillarum*                     **Former Breeder**
A rare spring (23 Apr–30 May) and fall (5 Jul–22 Oct) transient and rare to uncommon summer visitor.

**Breeding**: nested at Seaford, York 1949 & 1950; a colony was at College Creek, *James City* 1957-1966.

**Peak Count**: 163 at Hog Island, *Surry* 26 Jul 1986

**SBC**: 26 on 8 May 1994

**Gull-billed Tern** *Gelochelidon nilotica*
There are two records each of 2 birds at Hog Island, *Surry*: 5 May 1986 and 25 Jul 1995.

**Caspian Tern** *Hydroprogne caspia*
A common spring (17 Mar–21 May) and fall (2 Jul–15 Dec) transient and uncommon summer resident.

**Peak Count**: 832 at Hog Island, *Surry* 9 Sep 2011

**SBC**: 67 on 6 May 1979

**Black Tern** *Chlidonias niger*
A rare spring (11 May–6 Jun) and rare to uncommon fall (13 Jul–23 Sep) transient.

**Peak Count**: 175 from College Creek, *James City* post Tropical Storm Ernesto 2 Sep 2006

**SBC**: 7 on 11 May 1997

**Roseate Tern** *Sterna dougalli*
There is one record. One was off Cheatham Annex, *York* 4 May 1980.

**Common Tern** *Sterna hirundo*
A rare to uncommon spring (31 Mar–30 May) and fall (1 July–4 Nov) transient and rare to uncommon summer visitor.

**Peak Count**: 110+ from the Jamestown Ferry, *James City* 19 Jul 1995

**SBC**: 87 on 16 May 1999

### Forster's Tern *Sterna forsteri*

A common spring
(9 Mar–May) and fall
(13 Jul–Dec) transient
and uncommon sum-
mer and winter resident.

**Peak Count**: 302 at
Kingsmill, *James City*
15 Nov 1994

**CBC**: 254 on 16 Dec
2001

**SBC**: 116 on 7 May 1989

Barbara Houston

### Royal Tern *Thalasseus maximus*

A common spring (6 Mar–May) and fall (5 Jul–28 Nov) transient and summer
resident and rare early winter visitor.

**Peak Count**: 600 at Hog Island, *Surry* 27 Aug 1998

**CBC**: 2 on 20 Dec 1998

**SBC**: 267 on 1 May 1988

Barbara Houston

### Sandwich Tern *Thalasseus sandvicensis*

There are four records: one at Hog Island, *Surry* 18 Aug 1987; one at Hog Island,
*Surry* 28 Jul 1996; one at Scotland Wharf, *Surry* 25 May 1997; 4 at College Creek,
*James City* post Tropical Storm Ernesto 2 Sep 2006

### Black Skimmer *Rynchops niger*
A rare summer and early fall visitor 6 Jun–6 Sep.

**Peak Count**: 28 at Felgates Creek, York River, *York* 8 Jun 1982

### Rock Pigeon *Columba livia*                                        **Breeder**
A common permanent resident that has likely been present locally since colonial times.

**Breeding**: adult on nest 30 Jun

**CBC**: 423 on 19 Dec 2004

**SBC**: 375 on 6 May 1978

### African Collared-Dove *Streptopelia roseogrisea*        **Breeder**
There are two records. A pair nested off Jamestown Road near Lake Powell, *James City* circa 1–17 Mar 1972. At least 2 young were observed at that nest 15 Mar, one of which subsequently died. The fate of the second, which survived to near fledging, was unknown. An individual was at Kingsmill, *James City* 3 Jan 1993.

### White-winged Dove *Zenaida asiatica*
There are two records; one was in Chickahominy Haven, Lanexa, *James City* "late" Feb–18 Mar 2009; one was a fly-by at College Creek, *James City* 15 May 2011.

Bill Williams

### Mourning Dove *Zenaida macroura*                              **Breeder**
An abundant permanent resident and transient.

**Breeding**: nests with eggs 23 April–2 Jul

**Peak Count**: 1,000+ at Kingsmill, *James City* 6 & 25 Sep 1981

**CBC**: 450 on 20 Dec 1992

**SBC**: 339 on 6 May 1978

**Passenger Pigeon** *Ectopistes migratorius*                              **Extinct**
Historical evidence indicates this species was once abundant locally.

**Common Ground-Dove** *Columbina passerina*
There is one record of a single bird at Kingsmill, *James City* 21 Oct 1980.

**Yellow-billed Cuckoo** *Coccyzus americanus*                              **Breeder**
An uncommon transient and summer resident 23 Apr–24 Oct.

**Breeding**: nesting 12 Jun–7 Sep; fledged young at nest 19 Sep

**Peak Count**: 10 at Kingsmill, *James City* 7 Jul 1979

**SBC**: 40 on 6 May 1979

**Black-billed Cuckoo** *Coccyzus erythropthalmus*
A rare spring (22 Apr–25 May) and fall (17 Aug–29 Oct) transient and rare
summer resident. There are 4 summer reports including one singing repeatedly
28 Jun–7 Jul at Kingswood, *James City*; one seen and heard at Surrender Field,
Yorktown, *York* 12 Jul.

**SBC**: one on 3 May 1992

**Barn Owl** *Tyto alba*                              **Breeder**
A rare and declining permanent resident and transient. This species was last
recorded in 2005 (11 Apr and 16 Oct) at Mainland Farm, *James City*.

**Breeding**: eggs in nest 2 Apr; downy young 16 Jun. The last recorded nesting
was at Kingsmill, *James City* in 2004 where young in the nest were observed to
12 Jun.

**Eastern Screech-Owl** *Megascops asio*                              **Breeder**
A rare and localized permanent resident.

**Breeding**: occupied nest 13 Apr

**Peak Count**: 5 on Jamestown Island, *James City* 16 & 21 Feb 1985

**CBC**: 15 on 16 Dec 1979

**SBC**: 6 on 2 counts:  6 May 1979 and 29 Apr 1984

### Great Horned Owl *Bubo virginianus*                    **Breeder**

An uncommon permanent resident.

**Breeding**: incubating 2 Feb; young in nest to 21 Apr

**Peak Count**: 4 on Jamestown Island, *James City* 22 Oct 1995

**CBC**: 32 on 22 Dec 1996

**SBC**: 12 on 1 May 2005

Felice Bond

### Snowy Owl *Bubo scandiacus*

There are two records. "A large white owl, a rare avis for this part of the country, was shot by Gurley Waltrip several miles southeast of Williamsburg last Saturday [17 January 1931], the bird measured five feet from tip to tip of the wings. The Soft White feathers of the owl were marked by small bars of black. The feet including toes are completely covered with fine fur-like feathers, indicating that the owls habitat may have been in a colder part of the country. The owl was probably looking over this part of Virginia to see what was going on."* One was at Hog Island, *Surry* 8-11 Dec 1954.

*Virginia Gazette. 1931. White Owl Shot Near Archer's Hope. Friday edition, January 23, 1931

### Barred Owl *Strix varia*                    **Breeder**

An uncommon permanent resident.

**Breeding**: incubating 2 Mar

**Peak Count**: 5-an adult with 4 young at Kingsmill, *James City* 14 May 1982

**CBC**: 10 on 22 Dec 1985

**SBC**: 13 on 6 May 1979

Bill Williams

### Long-eared Owl *Asio otus*

There are three records: one at Yorktown, *York* 25 Feb 1951; one at Seaford, *York* 18 Mar 1952; 1–2 at Kingsmill, *James City* 19 Dec 1979–4 Jan 1980. This species likely occurs more frequently than current records indicate.

**Peak Count:** 2 at Kingsmill, *James City* 1 & 2 Jan 1980

### Short-eared Owl *Asio flammeus*

There are three records: one at Powhatan Creek, Colonial Parkway near Jamestown, *James City* 19 Mar 1987; 2 at Hog Island, *Surry* 20–26 Jan 1991; 2 at Hog Island, *Surry* 21 Dec 2008

**Peak Count:** 2 at Hog Island, *Surry* 20–26 Jan 1991 and 21 Dec 2008

**CBC:** 2 on 21 Dec 2008

### Northern Saw-whet Owl *Aegolius acadicus*

A rare winter visitor with nine records 6 Nov–9 Mar. Three of these records involved fresh carcasses. There have been no records since 1996.

**Peak Count:** 4 at College Woods, Williamsburg "early Feb" 1996

### Common Nighthawk *Chordeiles minor*

A rare spring (4 Apr–2 Jun) and fall (4 Aug–5 Nov) transient.

**Peak Count:** 25 over Queens Creek, *York* 29 Aug 1991

**SBC:** one on 3 counts: 3 May 1992; 8 May 1994; 29 Apr 2007

### Chuck-will's-widow *Anstrostomus carolinensis*          **Probable Breeder**

A rare transient and summer resident 23 Apr–16 Jul.

**Peak Count:** 4 at Camp Peary, *York* 2 May 2010

**SBC:** 7 on 5 May 1985

### Eastern Whip-poor-will *Anstrostomus vociferus*          **Probable Breeder**

A rare transient and summer resident 1 Apr–17 Sep.

**Peak Count:** 11 off Jolly Pond Road, *James City* 1 May 1988

**SBC:** 23 on 7 May 1989

### Chimney Swift *Chaetura pelagica*          **Breeder**

A common transient and summer resident 27 Mar–30 Oct.

**Breeding:** young in nest 5 Aug

**Peak Count:** 50 in Williamsburg 13 Apr 1981; 50 at Kingsmill, *James City* 26 Sep 1986

**SBC:** 117 on 6 May 1978

### Ruby-throated Hummingbird *Archilochus colubris* **Breeder**

A common transient and summer resident 4 Apr–11 Nov. There are two winter records, both confirmed by banding; one banded 28 Jan 2012 was present "late" Oct 2011 thru at least 12 Apr 2012.

**Peak Count**: 55 at a Queens Lake, *York* residence Jun–Jul 1993

**SBC**: 31 on 1 May 2011

### Rufous Hummingbird *Selasphorus rufus*

A rare and irregular late fall through winter visitor 24 Sep–8 Apr with six records confirmed by banding. A female visited a Settlers' Mill, *James City* feeder for 4 consecutive winters 2001–2004.

**Peak Count**: 3 banded 21 Jan 2002, all first winter females

**CBC**: one on 2 counts: 16 Dec 2001 and 14 Dec 2003

#### Rufous/Allen's Hummingbird *Selasphorus rufus/sasin*

There have been several reports of unidentified *Selasphorus sp.* Nov–early Jun.

### Belted Kingfisher *Ceryle alcyon* **Breeder**

An uncommon permanent resident.

**Breeding**: adults at nest sites as early as 1 Apr to as late as 20 May

**Peak Count**: 7 at Cheatham Annex, *York* 25 Oct 1984

**CBC**: 42 on 16 Dec 1984

**SBC**: 23 on 16 May 1999

Fred Blystone

### Red-headed Woodpecker *Melanerpes erythrocephalus* **Breeder**

An uncommon localized permanent resident and short distance transient.

**Breeding**: adults at nest sites as early as 10 Apr; feeding young at nest site to 25 Jun

**Peak Count**: 21 on Jamestown Island, *James City* 8 Jun 2008

**CBC**: 30 on 15 Dec 2002

**SBC**: 59 on 26 Apr 2009

### Red-bellied Woodpecker *Melanerpes carolinus*      **Breeder**

A common permanent resident.

**Breeding**: adults at nest site 14 Apr; fledged young by 25 May

**Peak Count**: 34 in the College of William and Mary woods, Williamsburg 11 Oct 1989

**CBC**: 140 on 19 Dec 2010

**SBC**: 147 on 1 May 2011

---

### Yellow-bellied Sapsucker *Sphyrapicus varius*

An uncommon transient and winter resident 26 Sep–8 May with an extreme date to 9 Jun.

**Peak Count**: 10 at Kingsmill, *James City* 21 Oct 1989

**CBC**: 46 on 17 Dec 1989

**SBC**: one on 3 counts:  2 May 1982; 29 Apr 1984; 8 May 1994

---

### Downy Woodpecker *Picoides pubescens*      **Breeder**

A common permanent resident.

**Breeding**: pair feeding downy young 24 May

**Peak Count**: 12 on Cheatham Annex, *York* 12 Sep 1982

**CBC**: 139 on 19 Dec 1982

**SBC**: 57 on 29 Apr 2012

---

### Hairy Woodpecker *Picoides villosus*      **Breeder**

An uncommon permanent resident.

**Breeding**: pair copulating 5 Apr; fledged young by 27 May

**Peak Count**: 7 on Hog Island, *Surry* 16 Jun 1974

**CBC**: 25 on 19 Dec 2010

**SBC**: 13 on 26 Apr 2009 and 1 May 2011

---

### Red-cockaded Woodpecker *Picoides borealis*

There is one record. One was off Dare Road, Yorktown, *York* 3 & 13 Feb 1985

## Northern Flicker *Colaptes auratus* **Breeder**

A common permanent resident and fall transient.

**Breeding**: feeding young at nest 15 May

**Peak Count**: 80 on Jamestown Island, *James City* 25 Sep 1988.

**CBC**: 195 on 16 Dec 1984

**SBC**: 64 on 5 May 1985


## Pileated Woodpecker *Dryocopus pileatus* **Breeder**

An uncommon permanent resident.

**Breeding**: nest with eggs 29 Apr

**Peak Count**: 5 in the College of William and Mary woods, Williamsburg 17 Dec 1989

**CBC**: 51 on 16 Dec 1990

**SBC**: 45 on 29 Apr 2012


## American Kestrel *Falco sparverius* **Breeder**

An uncommon to rare transient and winter and summer resident, recorded all months. Data from the College Creek Hawk Watch, *James City* indicate spring migration occurs 10 Feb–25 Apr with a peak circa 24 Mar.

**Breeding**: adults feeding fledglings 16 June

**Peak Count**: 24 at the College Creek Hawk Watch, *James City* 23 Mar 2003

**CBC**: 29 on 16 Dec 1979

**SBC**: 9 on 29 Apr 1984; recorded on only 8 SBCs since 1990


## Merlin *Falco columbarius*

A rare fall and spring transient and rare winter visitor 7 Sep–21 May. Data from the College Creek Hawk Watch, *James City* indicate spring migration occurs 20 Mar–8 May with a peak circa 25 Apr.

**Peak Count**: 5 at the College Creek Hawk Watch, *James City* 4 Apr 2012

**CBC**: 2 on 16 Dec 2001

**SBC**: one on 7 counts; most recently 26 Apr 2009

## Peregrine Falcon *Falco peregrinus*                    **Breeder**

A rare spring and fall transient and
rare winter visitor 19 Sep–17 May.

**Breeding**: Since 1987 this species
has nested near Kingsmill, *James City*
at the Moth Ball Fleet (technically
in the city of Newport News). One
to two birds occupied the Coleman
Bridge, Yorktown, *York* 1987–1991; a
pair fledged one of two young there
in 1991.

**Peak Counts**: 4 at the College Creek
Hawk Watch, *James City* 9 May 2006

Bill Williams

**CBC**: one on 4 counts-on the 1 Feb 1954 Yorktown CBC; on the Williamsburg
CBC 18 Dec 1983; 15 Dec 2002;
20 Dec 2011

**SBC**: one on 2 May 2002

## Carolina Parakeet *Conuropsis carolinensis*                    **Extinct**

There is compelling evidence this species was present locally during winter
months. Writing in 1612, William Strachey, who resided at Jamestown, offered
the following: "Parakitoes I haie seene many in the Winter and knowne divers
killed, yet be they a Fowle most swift of wing, their winges and Breasts are of a
greenish coulor with forked Tayles, their heades some Crymsen, some yellow,
some orange-tawny, very beautyfull, ..."

## Olive-sided Flycatcher *Contopus cooperi*

There are five records, all of single birds: Cheatham Annex, *York* 1 Jun 1980;
Jamestown Island, *James City* 27 May 1996; Chippokes Plantation State Park
swamp, *Surry* 18 May 1998; Greensprings Greenway Trail, *James City* 4 Sep
2000; Greensprings Greenway Trail, *James City* 3 Sep 2006

## Eastern Wood-Pewee *Contopus virens*                    **Breeder**

An uncommon transient and summer resident 18 Apr–14 Oct.

**Breeding**: adults feeding fledged young 19 Aug

**Peak Counts**: 12 at Cheatham Annex, *York* 1 Jun 1980; 10 at Kingsmill, *James City*
7 Sep 1981; 10 on Jamestown Island, *James City* 8 Sep 1995

**SBC**: 175 on 9 May 2004

## Yellow-bellied Flycatcher *Empidonax flaviventris*

A rare transient with eight records, 7 of which are fall (26 Aug–30 Sep).

**Peak Count**: 3 in the College of William and Mary woods, Williamsburg 21 Sep 1987

**SBC**: one on 16 May 1999

## Acadian Flycatcher *Empidonax virescens*                **Breeder**

A common transient and summer resident 24 Apr–16 Oct.

**Breeding**: incubating 28 May; adults feeding young in nest 14 Jun

**Peak Count**: 17 at York River State Park, *James City* 29 Jul 1979

**SBC**: 72 on 15 May 1983

## Willow Flycatcher *Empidonax traillii*

A rare and irregular spring (7 May–2 Jun) and fall transient with some 7–8 definitive records of singing individuals.

**Peak Count**: 3 on Jamestown Island, *James City* 15 May 1990.

**SBC**: one on 7 May 1989 and 4 May 2008

### Traill's Flycatcher (Willow/Alder) *Empidonax tralli/alnorum*

There are several reports of non-vocal *Empidonax* recorded as Willow/Alder Flycatchers 25 Aug–8 Oct.

**Peak Count**: 6 off Jolly Pond Road, *James City* 27 Sep 1991

## Least Flycatcher *Empidonax minimus*

There are three records: singles banded at the College of William and Mary Population Ecology Lab site, Williamsburg 28 Sep 1974 and 4 Sep 1975; one on Jamestown Island, *James City* 16 Sep 2011.

## Eastern Phoebe *Sayornis phoebe*                **Breeder**

An uncommon permanent resident and transient, becoming rare in winter.

**Breeding**: nest building 27 Mar; eggs by 13 Apr; incubating to 12 Jun

**Peak Count**: 5 in the College of William and Mary woods, Williamsburg 20 Oct 1989

**CBC**: 23 on 19 Dec 1993

**SBC**: 66 on 16 May 1999

## Ash-throated Flycatcher *Myiarchus cinerascens*

There is one record. One was at Cheatham Annex, *York* 17–20 Dec 1989.

**CBC**: one on 17 Dec 1989

### Great Crested Flycatcher *Myiarchus crinitus*      **Breeder**

A common transient and summer resident 15 Apr–2 Oct.

**Breeding**: nest building 11 May; fledged young by 19 Jun

**Peak Count**: 20 on Cheatham Annex, *York* 1 Jun 1980

**SBC**: 158 on 1 May 2011

### Western Kingbird *Tyrannus verticalis*

There are eight records, seven fall (7 Sep–30 Nov) and one late spring, the latter a single bird at Drummond's Field, *James City* 4 Jun 1984.

### Eastern Kingbird *Tyrannus tyrannus*      **Breeder**

A common transient and summer resident 27 Mar–6 Oct.

**Breeding**: nest building 16 May; incubating 2 Jun; feathered young in nest to 12 Aug

**Peak Count**: 100+ at College Creek, *James City* 1 Sep 2006 during Tropical Storm Ernesto

**SBC**: 176 on 15 May 1983

### Scissor-tailed Flycatcher *Tyrannus forficatus*

There are two records. An immature was at Hog Island, *Surry* 21 Jul 1994. An adult was at Tomahund Plantation, *Charles City* 0.9 miles west of the Chickahominy River 5 Jun 1988.

### Fork-tailed Flycatcher *Tyrannus savana*

There is one record, Virginia's first. One was at Tomahund Plantation, *Charles City* 0.9 miles west of the Chickahominy River 3 Jun–1 Aug 1988.

### Loggerhead Shrike *Lanius ludovicianus*      **Probable Breeder**

A formerly rare resident and transient, this species has not been recorded locally since one was at Hog Island, *Surry* 25 Aug 1989

**Breeding**: 1–3 birds at Hog Island, *Surry* throughout the summer of 1974 suggested breeding

**Peak Count**: 3 at Hog Island, *Surry* 12 and 26 Aug 1974

**CBC**: 2 on 2 counts: the 1 Jan 1954 and the 27 Dec 1954 Toano CBC

### Northern Shrike *Lanius excubitor*
There is one record, Virginia's second. One was banded at Queens Lake, *York* 5 Mar 1966.

### White-eyed Vireo *Vireo griseus* **Breeder**
An uncommon transient and summer resident (1 Apr–19 Oct) and rare winter visitor.

**Breeding**: nest with eggs 17 May; feeding young to 5 Jul

**Peak Count**: 18 at Charleston Heights, *York* 25 Apr 1982

**CBC**: one on 18 Dec 1988

**SBC**: 138 on 29 Apr 1984

### Yellow-throated Vireo *Vireo flavifrons* **Breeder**
An uncommon to rare transient and summer resident 16 Mar–2 Oct.

**Breeding**: nest building 3 May

**Peak Count**: 4 at York River State Park, *James City* 18 May 1996

**SBC**: 20 on 2 May 1982

### Blue-headed Vireo *Vireo solitarius*
A rare spring (3 Mar–6 Jun) and fall (30 Aug–9 Nov) transient and rare winter visitor.

**Peak Count**: 5 at York River State Park, *James City* 14 Feb 1992

**CBC**: one on 3 dates:  16 Dec 1990; 17 Dec 1991; 21 Dec 1997

**SBC**: 5 on 11 May 1997

### Warbling Vireo *Vireo gilvus*
There are nine records, all of single birds, for this rare spring (5–26 May) and fall (18 Aug and 3 Sep) transient and rare summer visitor.

### Philadelphia Vireo *Vireo philadelphicus*
A rare spring (23 Apr–21 May) and fall (9 Sep–14 Oct) transient.

**Peak Count**: 2 in Bassett Hall Woods, Williamsburg 26 Sep 1985

**SBC**: 2 on 11 May 1997

**Red-eyed Vireo** *Vireo olivaceus*                                          **Breeder**

A common transient and
summer resident 11 Apr–24 Oct.

**Breeding**: nest with young 7 Jul

**Peak Count**: 39 at York River State Park, *James City* 17 Jun 1992

**SBC**: 293 on 3 May 1987

Felice Bond

**Blue Jay** *Cyanocitta cristata*                                          **Breeder**

A common permanent resident and localized transient. "While the Blue Jay is
abundant at Richmond, it decreases rapidly eastward and is quite uncommon
at Williamsburg and rare in the Cape Henry region. Some increase has been
noted recently, however, and Grey found young on the wing at Williamsburg
June 6 and nest building June 16."*

**Breeding**: nest building 12 Apr; fledged young by 19 Apr; incubating 19 May

**Peak Count**: 75 on Jamestown Island, *James City* 25 Sep 1988

**CBC**: 261 on 17 Dec 1989

**SBC**: 149 on 1 May 1988

* Scott, F. R. 1951. Nesting season-1950-Virginia. Raven 22 (5 & 6): 29.

**American Crow** *Corvus brachyrhynchos*                                          **Breeder**

A common permanent resident.

**Breeding**: nest building as early as 27 Jan

**Peak Count**: 76 at Mill Creek, *James City* 5 Nov 2011

**CBC**: 438 on 21 Dec 1980

**SBC**: 223 6 May 1978

**Fish Crow** *Corvus ossifragus* **Breeder**

A common to locally abundant transient and summer resident and rare winter resident. Migrants typically arrive in early March.

**Breeding**: nest building 14 Apr; feeding young in nest 10 May; fledged young 30 Jun

**Peak Count**: a flock of up to 250 roosted at Kingsmill, *James City* during Dec 1980

**CBC**: 300 on 20 Dec 1981

**SBC**: 94 on 8 May 1994

**Common Raven** *Corvus corax*

There are three records, all of single birds: at Seaford, *York* 22 Jun 1949; over Interstate 64 near Camp Peary, *York* 22 Sep 1996; over Monticello Marketplace, *James City* 23 Apr 2010.

**Horned Lark** *Eremophila alpestris*

A rare to uncommon transient and winter visitor 23 Aug–14 Jun.

**Peak Count**: 40 along the Colonial Parkway, *James City* 12 Feb 1999

**CBC**: 45 on the 1 Jan 1954 Toano CBC

**SBS**: 2 on 28 Apr 1991

**Northern Rough-winged Swallow** *Stelgidopteryx serripennis* **Breeder**

An uncommon transient and summer resident 10 Mar–28 Sep. Spring migrants have been noted to 23 May. This species becomes scarce locally after mid-June.

**Breeding**: adults at nest sites by 18 Apr; feeding young 20 Jun

**Peak Count**: 20+ at Queen's Lake, *York* 15 Apr 1984

**SBC**: 86 on 4 May 1986

**Purple Martin** *Progne subis* **Breeder**

An uncommon to common transient and summer resident 9 Mar–21 Sep. This species has been declining locally since the 1990s.

**Breeding**: young in nest boxes 18 Jun

**Peak Count**: 3,500 at Yorktown, *York* 12 Aug 1979

**SBC**: 643 on 4 May 1986. Recent SBC counts have not exceeded 50.

**Tree Swallow** *Tachycineta bicolor*                                    **Breeder**

A common to abundant transient and summer resident (9 Mar–1 Nov) and uncommon to rare winter visitor. Spring migrants have been noted to 19 May.

**Breeding**: adults at nest site 7 Jun

**Peak Count**: 5,000 at College Creek, *James City* 14 Sep 1985

**CBC**: 18 on the 20 Dec 1950 Yorktown CBC

**SBC**: 1,213 on 1 May 1988

---

**Bank Swallow** *Riparia riparia*                                  **Former Breeder**

A rare to uncommon transient and summer resident 7 Apr–11 Sep. Spring migrants have been noted to 25 May. This species is occasionally locally common in late summer at Hog Island, *Surry* and on the Chickahominy River, *James City*.

**Peak Count**: 500 at Hog Island, *Surry* 4 Aug 1990; "dozens" at College Creek, *James City* 10 May 2010

**SBC**: 75 on 30 Apr 2006

---

**Cliff Swallow** *Petrochelidon pyrrhonota*                              **Breeder**

A rare spring (2–16 May) and fall (8 Jul–11 Sep) transient and rare summer resident. "A number of Cliff Swallows" were at Seaford, *York* 6 May 1934.*

**Breeding**: nesting at Little Creek Reservoir, *James City* 1994, 1995, 2009, 2010 and at Felgate's Creek, *York* 2005–2007

**Peak Count**: 6 at Little Creek Reservoir, *James City* 23 Jun 1995

**SBC**: 7 on 16 May 1999

*Unpublished field notes of F. M. Jones

---

**Cave Swallow** *Petrochelidon fulva*

There is one record of three birds at Mainland Farm, *James City* 17 Nov 2008.

---

**Barn Swallow** *Hirundo rustica*                                        **Breeder**

A common transient and summer resident 23 Mar–25 Sep (extreme date 12 Nov) and rare winter visitor.

**Breeding**: nest with downy young 17 Jun; incubating 24 Jun

**Peak Count**: 2,173 at Hog Island, *Surry* on the 30 Apr 2006 SBC

**CBC**: one on 17 Dec 1991

**SBC**: see above

## Carolina Chickadee *Poecile carolinensis* **Breeder**
A common permanent resident.

**Breeding**: nest building 9 Mar; incubating 3 Apr; fledged young by 28 Apr

**Peak Count**: 33 in the College of William and Mary woods, Williamsburg 4 Nov 1989

**CBC**: 391 on 19 Dec 1982

**SBC**: 230 on 29 Apr 2012

## Tufted Titmouse *Baeolophus bicolor* **Breeder**
A common permanent resident.

**Breeding**: incubating 24 Apr; fledged young by 20 May

**Peak Count**: 46 in the College of William and Mary woods, Williamsburg 20 Oct 1989

**CBC**: 273 on 19 Dec 1982

**SBC**: 229 on 29 Apr 2012

## Red-breasted Nuthatch *Sitta canadensis*
A rare and irregular transient and winter resident 9 Sep–13 May.

**Peak Count**: 6 York River State Park, *James City* 13 Nov 1991

**CBC**: 24 on 20 Dec 1981

**SBC**: 2 on 6 May 1978 and 3 May 1987

## White-breasted Nuthatch *Sitta carolinensis* **Breeder**
A common permanent resident.

**Breeding**: incubating 27 Mar; young in the nest by 7 Apr

**Peak Count**: 13 in the College of William and Mary woods, Williamsburg 11 Oct 1989

**CBC**: 194 on 16 Dec 2001

**SBC**: 37 on 1 May 2011

## Brown-headed Nuthatch *Sitta pusilla* **Breeder**
An uncommon, highly localized permanent resident.

**Breeding**: 1-egg nest 4 Apr

**Peak Count**: 22 at Hog Island, *Surry* 28 Jan 1981

**CBC**: 74 on 16 Dec 1984

**SBC**: 45 on 5 May 1985

**Brown Creeper** *Certhia americana*

An uncommon to rare transient and winter visitor 17 Sep–6 May.

**Peak Count**: 15–18 at Cheatham Annex, *York* 16 Oct 1983

**CBC**: 46 on 19 Dec 1982

**SBC**: one on 3 counts: 6 May 1979; 4 May 1980; 29 Apr 1990

**House Wren** *Troglodytes aedon* **Breeder**

An uncommon transient, rare winter resident, and common summer resident. Migrants arrive by 11 April with fall movement noted by early October.

**Breeding**: nest building 2 May to 7 Jul; fledged young by 13 Jun

**Peak Count**: 8 banded at the College of William and Mary Population Ecology Lab site, Williamsburg 24 Apr 1972

**CBC**: 9 on 19 Dec 2004

**SBC**: 31 on 3 May 1998

**Winter Wren** *Troglodytes hiemalis*

An uncommon transient and winter resident 10 Sep–1 May.

**Peak Count**: 12 at the College of William and Mary Population Ecology Lab site, Williamsburg 19 Nov 1989

**CBC**: 16 on 22 Dec 1996

**SBC**: one on 1 May 1988

**Sedge Wren** *Cistothorus platensis*

A rare transient and winter visitor 27 Sep–6 May

**Peak Count**: 2 at Hog Island, *Surry* 15 Mar 1992

**CBC**: 4 on the 23 Dec 1952 Yorktown CBC

**SBC**: one on 3 counts: 6 May 197; 1 May 1988; 29 Apr 2012

**Marsh Wren** *Cistothorus palustris* **Breeder**

A rare transient and resident, recorded all months. In spring 1959 John Grey found the marshes around Williamsburg "bare of Long-billed Marsh Wrens where they are normally abundant," possibly a result of the marsh vegetation being "severely beaten down by snow last winter, but even new growth had not brought the birds back."

**Breeding**: incubating 26 May

**Peak Counts**: 6 at Hog Island, *Surry* 15 May 1974; 6 at York River Sate Park, *James City* 7 May 1979; 10–12 Jamestown Island marshes, *James City* 2 Aug 1985.

**CBC**: 5 on 17 Dec 1989

**SBC**: 6 on 1 May 2005

**Carolina Wren** *Thryothorus ludovicianus*                    **Breeder**

A common permanent resident.

**Breeding**: nest building 3 Mar; egg laying 24 Mar; downy young in nest to 26 Aug

**Peak Count**: 32 in the College of William and Mary woods, Williamsburg 4 Nov 1989

**CBC**: 238 on 16 Dec 1984

**SBC**: 188 on 29 Apr 2012

---

**Bewick's Wren** *Thyromanes bewickii*

There is one record. One was banded at the College of William and Mary Population Ecology Lab site, Williamsburg 4 Oct 1975.

---

**Blue-gray Gnatcatcher** *Polioptila caerulea*                    **Breeder**

A common transient and summer resident (21 Mar–27 Sep) and rare fall and winter visitor.

**Breeding**: nest building 6 Apr

**Peak Counts**: 25–30 at Waller Mill Park, Williamsburg 28 Apr 1989; 35–40 at Hog Island, *Surry* 27 Jul 1993

**CBC**: one on 5 counts: 18 Dec 1983; 21 Dec 1986; 21 Dec 1997; 16 Dec 2001; 18 Dec 2011

**SBC**: 205 on 26 Apr 2009

---

**Golden-crowned Kinglet** *Regulus satrapa*

A common transient and winter resident 7 Oct–22 Apr.

**Peak Count**: 57 at York River State Park, *James City* 13 Nov 1991

**CBC**: 212 on 17 Dec 1989

---

**Ruby-crowned Kinglet** *Regulus calendula*

A common transient and winter resident 17 Sep–14 May

**Peak Count**: 12–15 near Jamestown, *James City* 14 Oct 1984

**CBC**: 266 on 16 Dec 1984

**SBC**: 41 on 5 May 1985

## Eastern Bluebird *Sialia sialis*                    **Breeder**

A common permanent resident and local transient.

**Breeding**: nest building 26 Feb; nests with eggs 20 Mar–3 Jul

**Peak Count**: 75-80 at Cheatham Annex, *York* 6 Nov 1983

**CBC**: 258 on 18 Dec 1983

**SBC**: 202 on 29 Apr 2012

Inge Curtis

---

## Townsend's Solitaire *Myadestes townsendi*

There is one record. A single bird, Virginia's second, was at Gilley Drive, Indigo Park, *James City* 1–29 Jan and 5–6 Apr 2008.

Joe Piotrowski

---

## Veery *Catharus fuscescens*

A rare to uncommon spring (28 Apr–28 May) and fall (23 Aug–22 Oct) transient. One was banded at the College of William and Mary Population Ecology Lab site, Williamsburg 10 Jun 1975.

**Peak Count**: 94 predawn at the Greensprings Greenway Trail, *James City* 25 Sep 2011

**SBC**: 14 on 2 counts:  15 May 1983 and 5 May 1996

---

## Gray-cheeked Thrush *Catharus minimus*

A rare to uncommon spring (26 Apr–4 Jun) and fall (17 Sep–24 Oct) transient.

**Peak Count**: 81 predawn at the Greensprings Greenway Trail, *James City* 7 Oct 2007

**SBC**: 10 on 5 May 1983

## Bicknell's Thrush *Catharus bicknelli*

A rare spring and fall transient. There are nine records for a total of 13 birds including the initial local report of one at Kingswood, *James City* 22 May 2001. All subsequent records are fall (28 Sep–14 Oct).

**Peak Count**: 3 predawn at the Greensprings Greenway Trail, *James City* 11 Oct 2009

## Swainson's Thrush *Catharus ustulatus*

A rare to uncommon spring (24 Apr–2 Jun) and fall (3 Sep–21 Oct) transient.

**Peak Count**: 31 predawn at the Greensprings Greenway Trail, *James City* 5 Oct 2008

**SBC**: 12 on 15 May 1983

## Hermit Thrush *Catharus guttatus*

An uncommon transient and winter resident 28 Sep–8 May.

**Peak Counts**: 50 near Yorktown, *York* following a 27 Feb 1950 snow event; 22 along Jolly Pond Road, *James City* following a 27 Feb 1997 snow event

**CBC**: 55 on 17 Dec 1989

**SBC**: 2 on 3 counts: 6 May 1978; 5 May 1985; 4 May 1986

## Wood Thrush *Hylocichla mustelina* **Breeder**

An uncommon transient and summer resident 31 Mar–22 Oct. This species has significantly declined since the 1990s. Recent spring bird counts have totaled <40.

**Breeding**: incubating 17 Apr; young in nest to 17 Jul

**Peak Count**: 30 at Camp Peary, *York* 4 Jul 1994

**SBC**: 112 on 6 May 1979

## American Robin *Turdus migratorius* **Breeder**

An abundant transient and winter and summer resident.

**Breeding**: nests with eggs from 14 Apr to 4 Jul

**Peak Count**: 50,000 in a Colonial Williamsburg roost 17 Jan 2006

**CBC**: 4,657 on 20 Dec 1981

**SBC**: 509 on 29 Apr 2012

**Gray Catbird** *Dumetella carolinensis*                    **Breeder**

A common transient and summer resident and rare winter resident.

**Breeding**: young in nest 7 Jun

**Peak Count**: 48 banded at College of William and Mary Population Ecology Lab site, Williamsburg 4 May 1972

**CBC**: 10 on 18 Dec 2005

**SBC**: 137 on 29 Apr 2012

---

**Northern Mockingbird** *Mimus polyglottis*                    **Breeder**

A common permanent resident.

**Breeding**: nest building 25 Mar; incubating 3 Apr; downy young 25 July

**Peak Count**: 25 at Kingsmill, *James City* 30 Aug 1982

**CBC**: 120 on 17 Dec 1989

**SBC**: 157 on 1 May 2011

---

**Brown Thrasher** *Toxostoma rufum*                    **Breeder**

An uncommon permanent resident and local transient.

**Breeding**: nest building 18 Mar–6 Jul; fledged young 4 May; young in nest 18 Jul

**Peak Count**: 35 on Jamestown Island, *James City* 17 May 1982

**CBC**: 35 on 19 Dec 2010

**SBC**: 105 on 29 Apr 2012

---

**European Starling** *Sturnus vulgaris*                    **Breeder**

An abundant permanent resident and common to abundant transient.

**Peak Count**: 432 at Drummond's Field, *James City* 15 Nov 2011

**Breeding**: nest building 7 Apr; feeding young at nest 12 May

**CBC**: 2,107 on 20 Dec 1981

**SBC**: 590 on 16 May 1999

## American Pipit *Anthus rubescens*

An uncommon to locally common transient and winter visitor 11 Nov–10 May.

**Peak Count**: 200 near Jamestown, *James City* 18 Jan 1985

**CBC**: 726 on 20 Dec 2009

**SBC**: 8 on 8 May 1994

Brian Taber

## Cedar Waxwing *Bombycilla cedrorum*      **Breeder**

A common to abundant transient and rare summer resident. A total of 1,292 deceased individuals were retrieved from a 1.9 km segment of Interstate 64 east of Williamsburg in *James City*, 23 Apr–7 May 2001 the result of traffic collisions as they fed at highway median plantings of thorny elegans (*Elaeagnus pungens*).

**Breeding**: fledged young 28 Jun and 15 Jul

**Peak Count**: 400 at Canterbury Hills, *James City* 16 Jan 1981

**CBC**: 1,300 on 16 Dec 2007

**SBC**: 534 on 2 May 1982

Inge Curtis

### Lapland Longspur *Calcarius lapponicus*

There are two records likely involving the same bird. One was seen near Archer's Hope, the Colonial Parkway, *James City* after a 29 Dec 1993 snow event. One was observed 12 & 13 Feb 1994 at College Creek, *James City* ~2 km from the 29 Dec 1993 observation.

### Snow Bunting *Plectrophenax nivalis*

There are nine records for this rare winter (5 Nov–13 Feb) visitor, including a male that was at the Colonial Parkway, Indian Field Creek pull-off, *York* 8 Jan–13 Feb 2002.

**Peak Count**: 7 on Jamestown Island, *James City* 20 Nov 1980

**CBC**: 2 on 20 Dec 1987

### Ovenbird *Seiurus aurocapilla*                                   **Breeder**

An uncommon transient and summer resident 31 Mar–20 Oct.

**Breeding**: a nest with eggs 30 Apr had hatchlings by 13 May

**Peak Count**: 11 at York River State Park, *James City* 13 May 1992

**SBC**: 120 on 6 May 1978

### Worm-eating Warbler *Helmitheros vermivorum*          **Possible Breeder**

A rare transient and summer resident 23 Apr–13 Sep. There is no confirmed breeding evidence for this species.

**Peak Count**: 4 at York River State Park, *James City* 13 May 1992

**SBC**: 7 on 4 May 2008

### Louisiana Waterthrush *Parkesia motacilla*                      **Breeder**

A rare to uncommon transient and summer resident 21 Mar–18 Sep.

**Breeding**: nest with young 7 May; carrying nest material 23 May

**Peak Count**: 5 at Camp Peary, *York* 14 June 1998

**SBC**: 30 on 2 May 1982

### Northern Waterthrush *Parkesia noveboracensis*

A rare to uncommon spring (18 Apr–11 Jun) and fall (23 Aug–16 Oct) transient.

One was banded at the College of William and Mary Population Ecology Lab site, Williamsburg 8 Aug 1974.

**Peak Counts**: 5 banded at the College of William and Mary Population Ecology Lab site, Williamsburg 13 May 1982; 5 at the Greensprings Greenway Trail, *James City* 24 Apr 2011

**SBC**: 9 on 4 May 1986

### Golden-winged Warbler *Vermivora chrysoptera*

A rare spring (25 Apr–6 May) and fall (30 Aug–24 Sep) transient with eleven records.

**Peak Count**: 3 at Queens Lake, *York* 29 Apr 1970

### Blue-winged Warbler *Vermivora cyanoptera*

A rare spring (23 Apr–19 May) and fall (11–26 Sep) transient.

**Peak Count**: 4–5 at Hollybrook/Kingswood, *James City* 30 Apr 1984

**SBC**: 18 on 2 May 1982

There are 2 records of single Brewster's Warblers, the Blue-winged Warbler × Golden-winged Warbler hybrid: at Barlow's Pond, *James City/York* 25 May 1990; at Tutter's Neck Pond, *James City* 5 & 6 May 1995.

There is one record of a single Lawrence's Warbler, the backcross between a first generation hybrid and a member of one of the parent species, at Jolly Pond, *James City* 28 & 29 Apr 1982.

### Black-and-white Warbler *Mniotilta varia*       **Breeder**

An uncommon spring (26 Mar–28 May) and fall (23 Aug–18 Oct) transient and rare winter visitor and summer resident.

**Breeding**: nest building 21 Apr; adults with fledged young 2 Jul

Territorial adults were found during the 2007 Virginia Society of Ornithology York River State Park Breeding Bird Foray.

**Peak Count**: 15 at York River State Park, *James City* 13 May 1992

**CBC**: 2 on 19 Dec 1999

**SBC**: 82 on 5 May 1985

### Prothonotary Warbler *Protonotaria citrea*       **Breeder**

An uncommon transient and summer resident 7 Apr–23 Sep.

**Breeding**: incubating 16 May & 16 Jun; fledged young to 4 Jul

**Peak Count**: 6 along Powhatan Creek, *James City* 1 Aug 1982

**SBC**: 26 on 29 Apr 2012

Inge Curtis

**Swainson's Warbler** *Limnothlypis swainsonii*

There are two confirmed records: one banded at Queen's Lake, *York* 3 Sep 1966; one banded at the College of William and Mary Population Ecology Lab site, Williamsburg 5 May 1975.

**Tennessee Warbler** *Oreothlypis peregrina*

A rare spring (30 Apr–6 Jun) and fall (31 Aug–16 Oct) transient.

**Peak Counts**: 3–4 Hollybrook/Kingswood, *James City* 10 May 1983; 4–5 at Kingswood, *James City* 13 Oct 1985

**SBC**: 2 on 5 May 1985

**Orange-crowned Warbler** *Oreothlypis celata*

A rare transient and winter visitor 5 Sep–25 Apr.

**Peak Count**: 3 on the 17 Dec 1991 **CBC**

**Nashville Warbler** *Oreothlypis ruficapilla*

A rare spring (29 Apr–15 May) and fall (30 Aug–9 Nov) transient and rare winter visitor. Winter records include one banded near Yorktown, *York* 23 Jan 1990.

**Peak Count**: 3 near Norge, *James City* 20 Sep 2012

**CBC**: one on 16 Dec 2007

**SBC**: 2 on 2 counts: 6 May 1978 and 29 Apr 1984

**Connecticut Warbler** *Oporornis agilis*

A rare transient. Thirteen of the 14 records occurred in the fall (9 Sep–8 Oct) including 3 banded at the College of William and Mary Population Ecology Lab site, Williamsburg. One was seen in the College of William and Mary Woods, Williamsburg 18 May 1967.

**Peak Count**: 2 at Hog Island, *Surry* 27 Sep 1995

**Mourning Warbler** *Oporornis philadelphia*

There are seven records, all of single birds. Five of these records are of individuals banded at College of William and Mary Population Ecology Lab site, Williamsburg 18–29 May (4) and 5 Sep (one). One was at Norge, *James City* 24 May 1953, and one was at the Greensprings Greenway Trail, *James City* 28 May 2000.

**Kentucky Warbler** *Oporornis formosus*                          **Breeder**

A rare and declining transient and summer resident 16 Apr–8 Oct.

**Breeding**: incubating 21 May

**Peak Count**: 4 at Cheatham Annex, *York* 7 June 1981

**SBC**: 24 on 15 May 1983

## Common Yellowthroat *Geothlypis trichas*     **Breeder**

A common transient and summer resident (2 Apr–4 Nov) and rare winter resident. This species has been recorded all months, with only one November record.

**Breeding**: adults feeding fledglings 5 Jun

**Peak Count**: 48 banded at College of William and Mary Population Ecology Lab site, Williamsburg 7 May 1975

**CBC**: 5 on 2 counts: 21 Dec 1980 and 20 Dec 1992

**SBC**: 132 on 11 May 2003

## Hooded Warbler *Setophaga citrina*     **Breeder**

A rare and declining transient and summer resident 12 Apr–14 Oct.

**Breeding**: incubating 11 May; feeding young 28 May; nest with young 22 Jun

**Peak Count**: 18 at Charleston Heights, *York* 25 Apr 1982

**SBC**: 73 on 2 May 1982

## American Redstart *Setophaga rusticilla*     **Breeder**

A common spring (13 Apr–10 Jun) and fall transient (17 Aug–29 Oct) and rare summer resident.

**Breeding**: nest building 31 May; female with brood patch banded at the College of William and Mary Population Ecology Lab site, Williamsburg 24 Jun 1978

**Peak Counts**: 20 at Cheatham Annex, *York* 28 Sep 1980 and 10 Sep 1981

**SBC**: 85 on 5 May 1983

## Cape May Warbler *Setophaga tigrina*

A rare spring (21 Apr–23 May) and fall (11 Sep–21 Oct) transient. Extreme dates include one banded at York River State Park, *James City* 2 Nov 1979 and one seen near Jolly Pond, *James City* 23 Nov 1989. There is a winter record of one on Jamestown Island, *James City* 19 Feb 1991.

**Peak Count**: 6 on Tyler Street, Williamsburg 13 Sep 1981

**SBC**: 4 on 5 May 1985

## Cerulean Warbler *Setophaga cerulea*

A rare spring (25 Apr–18 May) and fall (29 Sep) transient with thirteen records.

**Peak Count**: 2 at Queens Lake, *York* 29 Apr 1970

**SBC**: one on 2 counts: 3 May 1987 and 8 May 1994

**Northern Parula** *Setophaga americana* **Breeder**

An uncommon transient and summer resident (25 Mar–11 Nov) and rare winter visitor. One recovered at Jamestown, *James City* 19 Jan 1985 was subsequently released.

**Breeding:** incubating 4 May

**Peak Count:** 20+ at Queen's Lake, *York* 8 Oct 1983

**CBC:** one on 20 Dec 1998

**SBC:** 120 on 2 May 1982

**Magnolia Warbler** *Setophaga magnolia*

An uncommon spring (27 Apr–1 Jun) and fall (5 Sep–19 Oct) transient.

**Peak Count:** 6 at Queens Lake, *York* 2 & 7 Oct 1980

**SBC:** 12 on 15 May 1983

**Bay-breasted Warbler** *Setophaga castanea*

A rare spring (4–27 May) and fall (2 Sep–7 Oct) transient.

**Peak Count:** 2 at York River State Park, *James City* 22 May 1994

**SBC:** one on 2 counts: 5 May 1985 and 5 May 1996

**Blackburnian Warbler** *Setophaga fusca*

A rare spring (22 Apr–26 May) and fall (24 Aug–16 Oct) transient

**Peak Count:** 3 in the College of William and Mary Woods, Williamsburg 30 Aug 1990

**SBC:** 2 on 3 May 1987

**Yellow Warbler** *Setophaga petechia* **Probable Breeder**

A common transient and rare summer resident 21 Apr–21 Oct. This species is a rare winter visitor.

**Peak Count:** 8–10 at Cheatham Annex, *York* 7 May 1984

**CBC:** 2 on 19 Dec 2004

**SBC:** 45 on 4 May 1986

**Chestnut-sided Warbler** *Setophaga pensylvanica*

A rare spring (2–23 May) and fall (29 Aug–29 Sep) transient.

**Peak Count:** 5 at Norge, *James City* 10 Sep 2012

**SBC:** 6 on 11 May 1997

## Blackpoll Warbler *Setophaga striata*

A common spring (13 Apr–24 Jun) and rare to uncommon fall (12 Sep–20 Oct) transient.

**Peak Counts**: 25 at Mill Creek, Colonial Parkway, *James City* 21 May 1994; 8 in the College of William and Mary Woods, Williamsburg 11 Oct 1989

**SBC**: 104 on 11 May 2003

## Black-throated Blue Warbler *Setophaga caerulescens*

An uncommon spring (19 Apr–18 May) and fall (30 Aug–1 Nov) transient.

**Peak Count**: 10 at Hollybrook/Kingswood, *James City* 14 May 1993

**SBC**: 57 on 4 May 2008

## Palm Warbler *Setophaga palmarum*

A rare spring (6 Apr–10 May) and common fall (14 Sep–15 Nov) transient and rare winter resident. The current records do not delineate the local seasonal status of the eastern *S. p. palmarum* and western *S. p. hypochrysea* populations.

**Peak Count**: 30 at Kingsmill, *James City* 8 Oct 1980

**CBC**: 9 on 17 Dec 1991

**SBC**: 8 on 1 May 2005

## Pine Warbler *Setophaga pinus*      **Breeder**

A common transient and summer and winter resident.

**Breeding**: nest building 2 Apr; feeding recently fledged young 2 Aug

**Peak Counts**: 40 at Cheatham Annex, *York* 9 Sep 1984

**CBC**: 54 on 20 Dec 1981

**SBC**: 101 on 3 May 1987

## Yellow-rumped Warbler *Setophaga coronata*

An abundant transient and winter resident 19 Sep–18 May.

**Peak Count**: 879 at College Creek, *James City* 8 Nov 2008

**CBC**: 2,349 on 20 Dec 1998

**SBC**: 423 on 29 Apr 2001

An Audubon's Warbler *(S. c. auduboni)* was banded near Yorktown, *York* 4 May 1981.

**Yellow-throated Warbler** *Setophaga dominica*                    **Breeder**

An uncommon transient and summer resident (14 Mar–6 Oct) recorded all months except November. This species is a rare winter visitor.

**Breeding**: nest building 18 Apr; adult with fledged young 16 Jun

**Peak Count**: 15 on Jamestown Island, *James City* 21 Apr 1989

**SBC**: 90 on 1 May 2011

---

**Prairie Warbler** *Setophaga discolor*                    **Breeder**

An uncommon transient and rare to uncommon summer resident (3 Apr–9 Oct) and rare winter visitor.

**Breeding**: recaptured individuals at the College of William and Mary Population Ecology Lab site, Williamsburg, throughout summer months suggested breeding.

**Peak Counts**: 12 on three dates the most recent at the Vineyards, *James City* 6 May 1997

**CBC**: one on 2 counts: 18 Dec 1994 and 21 Dec 1997

**SBC**: 89 on 2 May 1982

---

**Townsend's Warbler** *Setophaga townsendi*

There is one record. An adult male was on the College of William and Mary campus, Williamsburg 8 Oct 2004.

---

**Black-throated Green Warbler** *Setophaga virens*

A rare spring (3 Apr–18 May) and fall (23 Aug–25 Oct) transient. Summer records include one banded near Yorktown, *York* 6 Aug 1977 and 2 seen at Deerwood Hills, *James City* 15 Jun 1988.

**Peak Counts**: 3 at Hollybrook/Kingswood, *James City* 4 Apr 1980; 4 at York River State Park, *James City* 17 Sep 1979

**SBC**: 7 on 3 counts: 9 May 2004; 4 May 2008; 26 Apr

---

**Canada Warbler** *Cardellina canadensis*

A rare spring (5–30 May) and fall (30 Jul–17 Oct) transient.

**Peak Counts**: 3 on three dates: 15 May 1984; 30 May 1985; 22 May 1995

**SBC**: 3 on 15 May 1983

---

**Wilson's Warbler** *Cardellina pusilla*

A rare spring (3–27 May) and fall transient (8 Sep–13 Oct).

**Peak Count**: 2 banded at College of William and Mary Population Ecology Lab site, Williamsburg 24 Sep 1981

**SBC**: one on 3 counts: 3 May 1992; 16 May 1999; 9 May 2004

## Yellow-breasted Chat *Icteria virens* **Breeder**

An uncommon transient and summer resident (6 Apr–20 Oct) and rare winter visitor.

**Breeding**: adult carrying food 13 June; adult feeding young 23 Jul

**Peak Count**: 14 banded at College of William and Mary Population Ecology Lab site, Williamsburg 7 May 1978

**SBC**: 42 on 15 May 1983

## Spotted Towhee *Pipilo maculatus*

There is one record, the first for Virginia; a male was at Barlow's Pond, *York/James City* 11–19 Feb 1995.

## Eastern Towhee *Pipilo erythrophthalmus* **Breeder**

A common permanent resident, transient, and winter resident.

**Breeding**: feeding fledged young 12 May to as late as 31 Aug

**Peak Count**: 23 on Jamestown Island, *James City* 19 Mar 2009

**CBC**: 137 on 17 Dec 1989

**SBC**: 145 on 1 May 2011

Bill Williams

## American Tree Sparrow *Spizella arborea*

A rare winter visitor 11 Nov–20 Feb.

**Peak Count**: 35 at Green Spring Plantation National Historic Site, *James City* during the winter of 1996

**CBC**: 5 on the 2 Jan 1956 Hog Island CBC

### Chipping Sparrow *Spizella passerina*  **Breeder**

A common transient and permanent resident. Migrant aggregations are evident mid-October–mid March.

**Breeding**: feeding young at nest 15 May

**Peak Count**: 55 at Greensprings Greenway Trail, *James City* 31 Dec 2006

**CBC**: 213 on 16 Dec 2007

**SBC**: 203 on 29 Apr 2012

### Clay-colored Sparrow *Spizella pallida*

There are two records, both of single birds at Mainland Farm, *James City*: 1–20 Jan and 6 Apr 2002; and 25 Sep 2011.

### Field Sparrow *Spizella pusilla*  **Breeder**

A common transient and uncommon summer resident.

**Breeding**: incubating 19 May

**Peak Counts**: 50 at the junc. of Route 199 and Route 5 (John Tyler Highway), *James City* 15 Jan 1979; 45 at the Williamsburg-Jamestown Airport, *James City* 20 Mar 1981

**CBC**: 328 on 18 Dec 1983

**SBC**: 46 on 1 May 1988

### Vesper Sparrow *Pooecetes gramineus*

A rare transient and winter visitor 6 Oct-23 May.

**Peak Counts**: 2 at Hog Island, *Surry* 7 Apr 1974 and 2 at Lafayette High School, *James City* 9 Apr 1980

**CBC**: 3 on 2 counts: 18 Dec 1977 and 17 Dec 1978

Brian Taber

### Lark Sparrow *Chondestes grammacus*

There are four records, all of single birds: at Hog Island, *Surry* 12 Aug 2000; at Jamestown High School, *James City* 23 Sep 2003; at Cheatham Annex, *York* 14 Dec 2003; at Mainland Farm, *James City* 27 Aug 2006.

**CBC**: one on 14 Dec 2003

## Savannah Sparrow *Passerculus sandwichensis*

A common to locally abundant transient and winter resident
12 Sep–24 May.

**Peak Count**: 100+ at Chippokes Plantation State Park, *Surry* 2 Feb 1994

**CBC**: 203 on the 2 Jan 1960 Hog Island, *Surry* CBC

**SBC**: 142 on 6 May 1978

There are three Ipswich Sparrow *(P. s. princeps)* records: one at Seaford, *York* 25 Nov & 2 Dec 1949 (bird was "collected" on this date); one at Yorktown, *York* 16 Feb 1952; one at Hog Island, *Surry* 17 Dec 2006.

## Grasshopper Sparrow *Ammodramus savannarum*     **Breeder**

A rare transient and summer resident (17 Apr–23 Oct) and rare winter visitor.

**Breeding**: birds singing on territory throughout the summer at several locations suggests local breeding

**Peak Count**: 9 near Lake Powell, *James City* 24 May 1967

**CBC**: one on the 28 Dec 1951 Yorktown CBC

**SBC**: 22 on 5 May 1985

## Henslow's Sparrow *Ammodramus henslowii*

There is one record of a single bird at Kingsmill, *James City* 28 Sep 1982.

## LeConte's Sparrow *Ammodramus leconteii*

There are three records for this late fall through early winter visitor: 1–2 at Drummond's Field, *James City* 29–30 Oct & 8 Nov 1992; one at College Creek, *James City* 19 Jan 1993; one at Mainland Farm, *James City* 27 Nov 2005 & 1 Jan 2006.

**Peak Count**: 2 at Drummond's Field, *James City* 29 Oct 1992

## Nelson's Sparrow *Ammodramus nelsoni*

A rare, highly localized spring transient and winter visitor 19 Nov–1 Jun.

**Peak Counts**: 3–4 at Queens Creek, *York* 17 May 1985; 2 at Seaford, *York* 19 Nov 2011

**Breeding**: a "Bishop's" Southern Sharp-tailed Sparrow at Seaford, *York* 14 Jun 1956 suggested (to the observers at the time) possible breeding

**CBC**: 2 at Hog Island, Surry 19 Dec 2004

**SBC**: 3 on 5 May 1985

Additional "Sharp-tailed Sparrow" reports of individuals not identified to species include one at York River State Park, *James City* 31 May 1979; one at College Creek, *James City* 12 & 14 Oct 1981; one at Hog Island, *Surry* 1 Jan 1986; 2 at Felgates Creek/Ringfield Picnic Area, *York* 11 Apr 1991.

**Seaside Sparrow** *Ammodramus maritimus*                    **Breeder**

A rare, very localized transient and summer resident 14 Apr–21 Oct. Winter records include one at Yorktown, *York* 2 Jan 1954.

**Breeding**: singing on territory throughout the summer

**Peak Count**: 12 on the Goodwin Islands, *York* 15 Jun 1992

**CBC**: 3 on the 1 Feb 1954 Yorktown CBC

**SBC**: 7 on 30 Apr 1995

**Fox Sparrow** *Passerella iliaca*

A rare transient and uncommon to rare winter resident 25 Oct–17 Apr.

**Peak Count**: 126 along the Colonial Parkway from College Creek to Jamestown Island, *James City* after a 17 Feb 2003 snow event

**CBC**: 52 on the 26 Dec 1947 Yorktown CBC

**Song Sparrow** *Melospiza melodia*                    **Breeder**

A common transient (22 Sep–1 Mar) and permanent resident.

**Breeding**:  incubating 24 Jun to as late as 16 Sep; tiny young in nest 26 Aug

**Peak Count**: 218 at Hog Island, *Surry* 6 Jan 1974

**CBC**: 1,032 on 20 Dec 1992

**SBC**: 80 on 29 Apr 1984

**Lincoln's Sparrow** *Melospiza lincolnii*

A rare spring (22 Mar–30 May) and fall (29 Sep–9 Nov) transient.

**SBC**: one on 4 May 1986

**Swamp Sparrow** *Melospiza georgiana*

An uncommon to locally common transient and common winter resident 10 Sep–28 May.

An immature was banded at the College of William and Mary Population Ecology Lab site, Williamsburg 15 Jun 1972.

**Peak Count**: 22 at the Greensprings Greenway Trail, *James City* 29 Oct 2000

**CBC**: 225 on 20 Dec 1992

**SBC**: 13 on 4 May 1986

Mike Powell

### White-throated Sparrow *Zonotrichia albicollis*

A common transient and winter resident 25 Sep–17 May (extreme date 28 May). An adult was at a McLaws Circle, *James City* feeder 17 Aug 1999.

**Peak Counts**: 100+ at Cheatham Annex, *York* 30 Jan 1982; 75 at Kingsmill, *James City* 11 Apr 1982

**CBC**: 1,192 on 18 Dec 1983

**SBC**: 279 on 26 Apr 2009

### White-crowned Sparrow *Zonotrichia leucophyrs*

A rare transient and winter resident 6 Oct–17 May.

**Peak Count**: 5 at Mainland Farm, *James City* 29 Oct 2006

**CBC**: 4 on 17 Dec 1989

**SBC**: 5 on 6 May 1978

### Dark-eyed Junco *Junco hyemalis*

A common transient and winter visitor 30 Sep–28 Apr. A partially leucistic (white-tailed) Pink-sided Junco (*J. h. mearnsi*) wintered in Windsor Forest, *James City* in 2012.

**Peak Count**: 105 at Deerwood Hills, *James City* 8 Mar 1989

**CBC**: 1,075 on 17 Dec 1989

**SBC**: 3 on 28 Apr 1991

A White-throated Sparrow × Dark-eyed Junco hybrid was at Cheatham Annex, *York* 9 May 2004.

### Summer Tanager *Piranga rubra*     **Breeder**

An uncommon transient and summer resident 17 Apr–9 Oct.

**Breeding**: incubating 10 Jun

**Peak Counts**: 12 at Cheatham Annex, *York* 22 May 1982; 6 at Hog Island, *Surry* 2 Sep 1974

**SBC**: 98 on 9 May 2004

Felice Bond

### Scarlet Tanager *Piranga olivacea*                    **Breeder**

An uncommon transient and summer resident 16 Apr–11 Oct.

**Breeding**: nest building 10 May

**Peak Count**: 14–16 in Bassett Hall Woods, Williamsburg 25 Sep 1985

**SBC**: 50 on 15 May 1983

### Western Tanager *Piranga ludoviciana*

There are six records all of single males 2 Dec–19 Apr; one was at Settlers' Mill, *James City* 6 Jan–27 Feb 2009 and 25 Jan–15 Mar 2010. The most recent record was a male at Settlers' Mill, *James City* 2 Dec 2011–14 Mar 2012.

Bill Williams

**CBC**: one on 18 Dec 2011

### Northern Cardinal *Cardinalis cardinalis*              **Breeder**

A common permanent resident sold during the colonial period as the Virginia Nightingale.

**Breeding**: nest building 16 Mar; incubating 9 Apr

**Peak Counts**: 50 on Cheatham Annex, *York* 2 Feb 1981;

**CBC**: 382 on 17 Dec 1989

**SBC**: 503 on 29 Apr 2012

### Rose-breasted Grosbeak *Pheucticus ludovicianus*

A rare spring (23 Apr–26 May) and fall (9 Sep–15 Oct) transient.

**Peak Count**: 20 at Queens Lake, *York* 25 Sep 1980

**SBC**: 21 on 29 Apr 2012

### Black-headed Grosbeak *Pheucticus melanocephalus*

There are three records, all of single birds: at Jamestown Farms, *James City* 13–14 Jan 1984; at Hog Island, *Surry* 19 Feb 1984; at Chisel Run, *James City* mid-Mar–4 Apr 1992.

## Blue Grosbeak *Passerina caerulea* **Breeder**

An uncommon spring and fall transient and summer resident 13 Apr–12 Oct (extreme date 23 Nov).

**Breeding**: nest building 2 May; adults carrying food to 30 Aug

**Peak Count**: 20 at Hog Island, *Surry* 13 Aug 1994

**SBC**: 42 on 3 May 1992

## Indigo Bunting *Passerina cyanea* **Breeder**

A common spring and fall transient and summer resident 3 Apr–23 Oct.

**Breeding**: downy young 15 Jun; incubating 7 Jul

**Peak Count**: 47 on Bushneck Road, *James City* 12 Oct 1991

**SBC**: 137 on 15 May 1983

## Painted Bunting *Passerina ciris*

Bill Williams

There are 10 records, all of birds at feeders: one male near Harwood's Mill Reservoir York 6 Jun 1952; one female in Marlbank, *York* 26 Mar–6 Apr 1983; one male in Kingsmill, *James City* 10–11 Jun 1989; a singing male at Kingsmill, *James City* 5 May 1990; one male at Shamrock Lane off Route 17 *York* 12 Dec 1990–18 Jan 1991; one male in Marlbank, *York* 13 Jan 1992; one male in Birchwood *James City* 1–11 Jan and 15 Feb 1997; one male in Norge, *James City* 20 Feb 1999; one male in First Colony, *James City* 24 Apr 2004; one male in Kingsmill, *James City* 17 Dec 2009–10 Feb 2010.

**CBC**: one on 20 Dec 2009

## Dickcissel *Spiza americana*

There are nine records, all of single birds, for this rare spring (16 Mar–24 May; extreme date 8 Jun) and fall (18 Sep–15 Oct) transient and rare winter visitor. One near Norge, *James City* 1 Jan 1954 was Virginia's first winter record.

**Peak Count**: 2 near the Williamsburg Lodge, Williamsburg during the winter of 1964

**Bobolink** *Dolichonyx oryzivorus*

A common spring (26 Apr–29 May) and fall (15 Jul–18 Oct; extreme dates 4 Jul and 18 Nov) transient. A singing male was at Hog Island, *Surry* 16 Jun 1974.

**Peak Count**: 2,500 at Hog Island, *Surry* 15 Sept 1988

**SBC**: 671 on 2 May 1982

**Red-winged Blackbird** *Agelaius phoeniceus*　　　　　　　　　**Breeder**

An abundant fall and spring transient and common to abundant summer and winter resident.

**Breeding**: incubating 19 May; feeding nestlings 26 Jul

**Peak Count**: 170,000 at Hog Island, *Surry* 22 Dec 1953

**CBC**: 386,647 on 20 Dec 1981

**SBC**: 1,422 on 1 May 1988

Inge Curtis

**Eastern Meadowlark** *Sturnella magna*　　　　　　　　　**Breeder**

An uncommon local resident and transient. This formerly common species has declined significantly since the 1990s.

**Breeding**: adult with recently fledged young 7 June

**Peak Count**: 50 at Kingsmill, *James City* 29 Nov 1980

**CBC**: 296 on 17 Dec 1978

**SBC**: 118 on 3 May 1987

### Yellow-headed Blackbird *Xanthocephalus xanthocephalus*

There are four records, all of single birds: in Toano, *James City* 10 Dec 1982; at Hog Island, *Surry* 5 May 1986; in Gate House Farms, *James City* 23 Mar 2003; in Kingsmill, *James City* 21 Apr 2007.

### Rusty Blackbird *Euphagus carolinus*

A rare and significantly declining transient and winter resident 8 Oct–16 May.

**Peak Count**: 450 at Queens Lake, *York* 28 Nov 1979

**CBC**: 92 on 19 Dec 2004

**SBC**: 129 on 29 Apr 1984

### Brewer's Blackbird *Euphagus cyanocephalus*

There are four records: 2 at Kingsmill, *James City* 3–5 Apr 1993; one female at Drummond's Field, *James City* 22 & 24 Mar 1994; one male at Mainland Farm, *James City* 13 Nov 2009; and…

**CBC**: one on 17 Dec 2000 at Hog Island, *Surry*

### Common Grackle *Quiscalus quiscula*        Breeder

An abundant transient and summer resident. Both *stonei* and *versicolor* subspecies have been documented; definitive seasonal occurrence for each is unclear.

**Peak Count**: ~1,000,000 passing over Colonial Williamsburg 24 Nov 2011

**Breeding**: nest building 28 Apr

**CBC**: 601,333 on 18 Dec 1994

**SBC**: 555 on 1 May 1988

### Boat-tailed Grackle *Quiscalus major*        Breeder

A rare, highly localized late winter visitor and spring and summer resident along the York River at Felgates Creek, Indian Fields Creek and on the Goodwin Islands, *York* 5 Feb–11 Nov. Four *James City* records include a male at Hollybrook/Kingswood 29 Mar 1986; 2 near Jamestown Island 1 May 2005; a male at the Jamestown Island causeway 18 Apr 2008; 2 males at College Creek 24 May 2009. Three Hog Island, *Surry* records include a female 30 Apr 1995; a female 9 May 2004; one male, one female 26 Apr 2009.

**Breeding**: nest building 12 Apr

**Peak Count**: 53 on the Goodwin Islands, *York* 15 Jun 1992

**SBC**: 9 on 11 May 2003

## Shiny Cowbird *Molothrus bonariensis*

There is one record, Virginia's first. A male was at the junction of Routes 634 and 633, *Surry* 18-27 Aug 1996.

## Brown-headed Cowbird *Molothrus ater*     **Breeder**

A common to abundant transient and winter and summer resident.

Locally documented host species include Eastern Phoebe, Great Crested Flycatcher, White-eyed Vireo, Red-eyed Vireo, Eastern Bluebird, Wood Thrush, Prothonotary Warbler, Yellow-breasted Chat, Eastern Towhee, Chipping Sparrow, Song Sparrow, Northern Cardinal, Indigo Bunting, Baltimore Oriole, House Finch.

**Peak Count**: 50,000 at Chippokes State Park, *Surry* 14 Dec 1996

**CBC**: 10,000 on the 22 Dec 1952 Yorktown CBC

**SBC**: 203 on 3 May 1992

Seig Kopinitz

## Orchard Oriole *Icterus spurius*     **Breeder**

An uncommon spring and fall transient and summer resident 13 Apr–15 Sep (extreme date 20 Oct).

**Breeding**: nest building 6 May

**Peak Count**: 14 at the Williamsburg-Jamestown Airport, *James City* 26 Jun 1981

**SBC**: 100 on 9 May 2004

## Baltimore Oriole *Icterus galbula*          **Breeder**

An uncommon transient (mid-Apr–17 May; 13 Aug–26 Sep; extreme date 18 Nov) and winter resident. This species has been recorded every month except October.

**Breeding**: 2 confirmed records both from Kingsmill, *James City*; nest building 10 May; fledged young by 5 Jun

**Peak Counts:** 9 on Virginia Avenue, Williamsburg 22 Feb 1978; 9 at Kingsmill, *James City* 18 Nov 1983

**CBC**: 15 on 21 Dec 1980—the national high for the 1980–81 CBC count season.

**SBC**: 12 on 9 May 1981

Joe Piotrowski

## Purple Finch *Haemorhous purpureus*

A rare to uncommon transient and winter resident 19 Oct–16 May. One banded 25 Jul 1964 at Westpoint, MA was recovered in Williamsburg 24 Mar 1966.

**Peak Count**: 75 at York River State Park, *James City* 25 Apr 1982

**CBC**: 155 on 19 Dec 1982

**SBC**: 8 on 2 May 1982

## House Finch *Haemorhous mexicanus*          **Breeder**

First recorded locally 16 Jan 1967, this species is now a common permanent resident and uncommon fall and spring transient.

**Breeding**: nest building 18 Mar; 3-egg nest 25 Mar; nest with young 3 Aug

**Peak Count**: 163 at the Greensprings Greenway Trail, *James City* 25 Nov 2001

**CBC**: 389 on 17 Dec 1989

**SBC**: 250 on 8 May 1994

## Red Crossbill *Loxia curvirostra*

There are three records all from 4 Mar–28 Apr 1976.

**Peak Count**: 12 at Lafayette High School, *James City* 28 Apr 1976

**Common Redpoll** *Acanthis flammea*

A rare, highly irregular winter visitor 10 Feb–23 Mar. Five of the ten records occurred during the winter of 1978.

**Peak Count**: 3 at Kingsmill, *James City* 18 Feb 1978

**Pine Siskin** *Spinus pinus*

Formerly a common to abundant transient and winter resident, this species is now rare to uncommon 14 Oct–13 May. One lingered at a *James City* feeder through June in 1989.

**Peak Count**: 100 at Gospel Spreading Farm, Colonial Parkway, *James City* 23 Dec 1985

**CBC**: 47 on 23 December 1952 Yorktown CBC

**SBC**: 71 on 4 May 1986

**American Goldfinch** *Spinus tristis*                    **Probable Breeder**

A common to abundant transient and resident.

**Peak Count**: 148 at the Greensprings Greenway Trail, *James City*  11 Nov 2007

**CBC**: 373 on 19 Dec 1982

**SBC**: 602 on 2 May 1982

**European Goldfinch** *Carduelis carduelis*

One was photographed in Williamsburg 30 Aug 1999.

**Evening Grosbeak** *Coccothraustes vespertinus*

Formerly a common to abundant transient and winter resident 29 Oct–29 May, this species is now a very rare and irregular winter transient. One banded at Queens Lake, *York* 2 Mar 1969 was recovered 15 May 1969 in Schenectady, NY; 1,720 were banded at Queens Lake, *York* 12 Jan–3 Apr 1970.

**Peak Counts**: 500 at Cheatham Annex, *York* "early Feb" 1952; 75 at Hollybrook/Kingswood, *James City* 6 Feb 1984

**CBC**: 76 on 17 Dec 1983

**SBC**: 64 on 29 Apr 1984

**House Sparrow** *Passer domesticus*                    **Breeder**

A common permanent resident.

**Breeding**: nest with young 26 Apr; feeding young at nest 9 Jul

**CBC**: 330 on 18 Dec 1977

**SBC**: 315 on 6 May 1978

# Contributors

David Abbott
Don Ackert
Marilyn & John Adair
W. Adair
Bob Ake
Jorn Ake
Bill Akers
Amanda Allen
Dave Anderton
Joy Archer
Tom Armour
Martha Armstrong
Scotty & John Austin
H. H. Bailey
Paul Baker
Pete Baril
Hugh Beard
Raymond Beasley
Ruth Beck
Ann Beckley
Meredith & Lee Bell
Louise Bethea
Henry Bielstein
Thom Blair
Fred Blystone
Mike Boatwright
Marge Boggs
Kay Boldt
Catherine Bond
Gordon Bond
Jim Booth
Arun Bose
Virginia & George Boyles
Dana Bradshaw

Rob Breeding
Martha Briggs
Ned Brinkley
Patrick Brisse
Mike Britten
John Broadwater
Chris Brown
Peter Brown
Bob Bruce
David Bryan
John Bryant
John Buck
Paul Buckley
Ryan Burdge
Rita Burris
Mitchell Byrd
Adam Byrne
Paul Cabe
Elsie Chapman
Jos Churan
Mrs. Frank Claiborne
David Clark
Linda Cole
Randy Coleman
Ann Condon
Ben Copeland
Valerie & George Copping
Tony Costillo
Jane Craig
Dan Cristol
Bob Cross
Bland Crowder
Andrew Curtis
Thelma Dalmas

Bertha Daniel
Evangeline Davis
Howard Davis
Fenton Day
Scott Dean
Henry DeGraf
Shirley & Steve Devan
John Dillard
Adam D'Onofrio
Grace & Joe Doyle
Mike Duffy
Juel Duke
Paul Dulaney
Paul DuMont
Kyle Dupuis
Joan Dutton
Barry Easley
Ward Ellis
Barbara Ema
Elisa Enders
Frank Evans
Peg Evans
John Faragher
Bettye Fields
Lon Fisher
Nicholas Flanders
Cindy Fletcher
Ed Flory
Bill Fortner
Gary Friedhaber
Paula Frohring
Walt Fuerer
Hans Gabler
Joe Garvin

Geoff Giles
Benny Gilliam
Chris Glasgow
Paul Glass
R. A. Glassell
Rich Goll
John Grey
Jack Gross
Vickie Gullet
Mary Gustafson
Charlie Hacker
W. J. Hadden
Gustav Hall
Eric Hamilton
Gary Hammer
Sam Hart
Bill Haywood
Ray Heath
Matt Henderson
Cathy Henning
Jose Hernandez
Eleanor & John Hertz
Dave Hewitt
Frank Hill
Bill Hines
Dick Hines
Bill Holcombe
Julie & Charles (Ty) Hotchkiss
Barbara Houston
Robert Huggett
David Hughes
Tom Hunter
Helen Irving
Mike Iwanik
Fred M. Jones

Homer Jones
Leigh Jones
Richard Joosten
Teta Kain
Norma & Ed Katz
Karen Kearne
Frances Keilocker
Bob Kennedy
Val Kitchens
Mary Ann Koeneke
Alice & Seig Kopinitz
Glenn Koppel
Pat and Allen Larner
Mark Lassiter
Dave & Phyllis Lee
William Leigh
Sara Lewis
Henry Lindsey
Jon Little,
Jan Lockwood
Bob & Cynthia Long
Carolyn Lowe
Joe Lowry
Larry Lynch
Dick Mahone
David Martin
Buddy Matthews
Bill Maye
Paul & Carol McAllister
Robert McCartney
Dawn McClaren
John McCloskey
Andy McGann
Elaine Mertus
Kathi & Mac Mestayer

Cathy Millar
Gregory Millslagle
Alex & Mike Minarik
John Minor
W. (Bill) F. Minor
Maryella Mitchell
Dorothy & Mike Mitchell
Pam Mitchell
Terry Moeslein
David Monahan
Thomas Moore
Bob Morris
Duryea Morton
Louise Moulds
Peggy Mylum
Jeanette Navia
Annie Newman
Charles Nimmo
Tim O'Connell
Grant Olsen
Joey Olszewski
Carol O'Neil
Brian Patteson
Judy & Joe Pauley
Bart Paxton
Dick Peake
Bruce Peterjohn
Mary & Lyman Peters
Sandy Peterson
Burdick Pierce
Harding Polk
Michael Powell
Susan Powell
Alex Powell
Mike Purdy

Mary Pulley
John Randolph
Everett Raynes
Steve & Shaun Reams
Bruce Reid
Larry Ricketts
Sue Ridd
Jim Rodgers
V. A. Rose
Chuck Rosenberg
Steve Rottenborn
Betsy Rozzell
Hugh Rutledge
Ineke & Donald Schaller
Dave Schantz
Virginia & Mel Schiavelli
Lee & Dave Schuster
Don Schwab
Bruce Schweitzer
Fred Scott
Pat Sgrinia
Emily Sharrett
Bill Sheehan
Sylvia Shirley
Dave Shoch
Dot Silsby
Zelda Silverman
Bart Singer
Claude Slauson
Anne Smith
Charley Smith
Fletcher Smith
Gary Smith
Ninna Snead
Bill Snyder

Dave Sobal
Alice & Dick Springe
Charles Steirly
Carol Stephens
Charles Stevens
Martha Stevens
Chris Stinson
Mike Stinson
Randy Strickland
Marg Strong
Susan Sturm
Brian Taber
Haskell Taylor
Joshua Taylor
Wes Teets
Brenda Tekin
Becky & Bill Tettway
Jewel Thomas
Mrs. T. P. Thompson
Gale Treiber
Jennifer Trevino
Tina Trice
Barry Trott
Roy Trow
Craig Tumer
Fitz Turner
David Tuttle
Jerry Via
Mrs. R. P. Wallace
Mack Walls
Gurley Waltrip
Bryan Watts
Valerie Weiss
Phil West
Dave Whelan

Ariel White
Dorothy Whitfield
Alex Wilke
Lou Wilkerson
Arlene Williams
Betty Williams
Bill Williams
Gary Williamson
Jack Willis
John Willis
Mike Wilson
Tom Wood
Suzie Woodall
Dave Worley
Dave Youker
Marilyn Zeigler

# Birding Locations

Virginia's Colonial Historic Triangle offers an enticing diversity of birding opportunities. The area's national, state, and local parks provide access to mature deciduous forests, multi-stage successional growth, fresh water impoundments and swamps, and the full spectrum of the Chesapeake Bay's tidal estuaries and wetlands.

The following is a list of publically accessible birding sites by jurisdiction.

## James City County

### Diascund Reservoir

This 1,110-acre reservoir is situated northwest of Williamsburg along the New Kent County/James City County line.

### Little Creek Reservoir Park

Located near Toano this 996-acre reservoir is a James City County public recreation facility with canoe and small boat facilities and trails through mixed deciduous forest.

### Jolly Pond

Jolly Pond is a former mill pond located along Jolly Pond Road, Route 633.

### York River State Park

Located off Riverview Road, route 606, in the northwest corner of James City County, this 2,550- acre facility is destination **CLP01** on the Virginia Birding and Wildlife Trail. An extensive trail system allows access to secondary growth and mature deciduous forests, a fresh water pond, tidal salt marsh, with viewpoints for the York River. A canoe/kayak launch is available.

### Freedom Park

Freedom Park is a 676-acre James City County multiple use facility located at the junction of Longhill Road, Route 612, and Centerville Road, Route 614.

### The Virginia Capital Trail

The Virginia Capital Trail is a paved bicycle and pedestrian trail that traverses from Jamestown to the Chickahominy River primarily along John Tyler Highway, Route 5.

### Chickahominy River

The Chickahominy River is a tributary of the James River northwest of Williamsburg. The river separates James City County from Charles City County and New Kent County.

## Chickahominy Riverfront Park

This is destination **CPL13** on the Virginia Birding and Wildlife Trail. It is a James City County managed 140-acre multiple-use facility located on John Tyler Highway, Route 5, immediately before the Judith Dresser Bridge. It may also be accessed from the Virginia Capital Trail. A canoe/kayak and boat launch are available.

## Greensprings Greenway Trail

The Greensprings Greenway Trail is destination **CLP02** on the Virginia Birding and Wildlife Trail. This public hiking/jogging facility encircles an ephemeral wetland. It may also be accessed from the Virginia Capital Trail.

## Powhatan Creek

This tributary of the James River meanders north from Jamestown Island towards its Longhill Swamp headwaters. A canoe/kayak launch is located off Jamestown Road, Route 31, across from Cooke's Nursery.

## Powhatan Creek Trail

This spur of the Virginia Capital Trail passes through a bald cypress wetlands behind Clara Byrd Baker Elementary School, at the Five Forks intersection of Ironbound Road and John Tyler Highway, Route 5.

## Jamestown

Jamestown is destination **CLP03** on the Virginia Birding and Wildlife Trail. Several birding sites are encompassed within the "Jamestown" complex including Jamestown Settlement, the Jamestown/Scotland Wharf ferry, and the National Park Service's Historic Jamestowne on Jamestown Island. It may also be accessed from the Virginia Capital Trail.

## Drummond's Field/Carlton Farms

Drummond's Field/Carlton Farms is located near Jamestown along Greensprings Road, Route 614. It may be accessed from the Virginia Capital Trail.

## Mainland Farm

Mainland Farm is immediately across Greensprings Road, Route 614, from Drummond's Field/Carlton Farms. It may be accessed from the Virginia Capital Trail.

## Green Spring Plantation National Historic Site

This 200-acre site located near the junction of Route 614, Centerville Road, and John Tyler Highway, Route 5, is owned and managed by the National Park Service. Public access is limited.

## Williamsburg-Jamestown Airport

This privately owned and operated airport is located off Lake Powell Road, Route 618, and is adjacent to the upper reaches of College Creek.

**Williamsburg Winery**

The Williamsburg Winery is located on Wessex Hundred Road off Lake Powell Road, Route 618, and also borders College Creek.

**Treasure Island Road**

Treasure Island Road, Route 617, an extension of Lake Powell Road, Route 618, traverses through a maturing deciduous forest and cropland to the Gospel Spreading Farm.

**Lake Powell**

Jamestown Road, Route 31, crosses this body of water. Viewing access is limited.

## City of Williamsburg

**College of William and Mary Population Ecology Lab site**

This site located off South Henry Street, Route 132, is adjacent to the current Marshall Wythe Law School.

**College Landing Park**

Located on South Henry Street this passive park provides a lookout tower and a marsh walkway overlooking one end of College Creek.

**Tutter's Neck Pond**

This small former mill pond is located off Quarter Path Road, Route 637, which connects Route 199, Humelsine Parkway, and Route 60.

**College of William and Mary Woods**

This deciduous forest adjacent to the College of William and Mary campus surrounds Lake Matoaka and forms the core of a 900-acre research/recreation preserve.

**Bassett Hall Woods**

Bassett Hall Woods is a 585-acre deciduous forest tract behind Bassett Hall, the former home of John D. Rockefeller, Jr. It is located off Francis Street in Colonial Williamsburg.

## York County

**Waller Mill Park**

Located on Airport Road, Route 645, between I-64 and Route 60 West, this 2,705 acre public facility surrounds the City of Williamsburg's 286-acre reservoir. The park's trails wind through a mature deciduous forest. Canoe and small boat rentals are available in season.

**Queens Lake and the Queens Lake Marina**

Queens Lake is a residential neighborhood located off the Colonial Parkway or at the end of Hubbard Lane, Route 716. The community surrounds Queens Lake, a former mill pond, and is bordered to the north by Queens Creek.

**New Quarter Park**

This 545-acre multiple use facility located at the terminus of Lakeshead Drive adjacent to the Queens Lake residential community is bordered by Queens Creek and Cub Dam Creek. A canoe/kayak launch is available.

**Fusiliers Redoubt**

This historical site, across from the Yorktown Victory Center on Old Williamsburg Road, offers views of the York River into Gloucester.

**Yorktown Waterfront**

Several access points here offer views of the mouth of York River towards the Chesapeake Bay

**Yorktown Victory Monument**

This site off Main Street in Yorktown offers views of the mouth of the York River.

**Yorktown Battlefield**

Historic Yorktown Battlefield is destination **CLP05** on the Virginia Birding and Wildlife Trail. There is a roadway system throughout the battlefield complex that passes through secondary growth deciduous forest and Surrender Field.

**Redoubts 9 & 10**

These Yorktown Battlefield sites offer views of the mouth of the York River.

**Beaverdam Creek**

This stream at the northeast end of Lee Hall Reservoir penetrates into southeastern York County. A large Great Blue Heron/Great Egret nesting site is located at the end of the creek drainage.

**Grafton Ponds Natural Area Preserve**

This unique 325-acre Virginia natural preserve is bisected by Fort Eustis Boulevard, Route 105, near the entrance to the Newport News Golf Club at Deer Run, part of Newport News Park. One portion of the preserve adjoins Warwick Road in the Park.

**Goodwin Islands**

This 377-acre saltmarsh at the mouth of the York River is destination **CLP06** on the Virginia Birding and Wildlife Trail. Access is by permit through the Chesapeake Bay National Estuarine Research Reserve at the Virginia Institute of Marine Science.

### Harwood's Mill Reservoir

This 265-acre reservoir is located off George Washington Highway, Route 17, in Grafton. Public access is available from Oriana Road.

## The Colonial National Parkway

The Colonial National Parkway, destination **CLP04** on the Virginia Birding and Wildlife Trail, is a 23-mile roadway connecting Yorktown and Jamestown passing through (actually beneath) the City of Williamsburg. The Parkway's numerous pull-offs and overlooks on both the York River and James River offer productive birding opportunities.

From Yorktown the following are excellent birding stops.

### Indian Field Creek

There are two pull-offs at distance marker K 7 that provide access to the York River and a tidal salt marsh.

### Felgates Creek

The two pull-offs at distance marker K 9 present broad vistas of the York River

### Jones Mill Pond

This overlook on to a former mill pond is located at distance marker K 15.

### College Creek

There are two College Creek pull-offs at distance markers K 26 and K 27, respectively. One near K 26 fronts the James River with views southeast towards the tip of Hog Island Wildlife Management Area in Surry County. This is the site of the College Creek Hawk Watch, which is active February through late May. The second pull-off faces College Creek and its brackish water marsh.

### Archers Hope

This pull-off at distance marker K 29 fronts the James River with views southeast towards Hog Island Wildlife Management Area in Surry County.

### Mill Creek

At distance marker K 31, this overlook faces across the Thoroughfare towards the southeastern end of Jamestown Island.

### Gospel Spreading Farm

Located at distance marker K 30, this 1100-acre active agricultural and dairy farm is privately owned.

### Powhatan Creek Overlook

This pull-out immediately across from the Historic Jamestowne entry offers a view of Powhatan Creek and its marshes.

## Surry County

### Hog Island Wildlife Management Area

Hog Island Wildlife Management Area is destination **CTW04** on the Virginia Birding and Wildlife Trail. The bird sightings credited to Hog Island, Surry came from the Hog Island tract of the larger Hog Island Wildlife Management Area complex.

> **Note to visitors:** The entry road to the Hog Island Wildlife Management Area passes through the Surry Nuclear Power Station facility. **ALL** vehicles **MUST** pass through a security check before proceeding to Hog Island. **ALL** persons desiring access to Hog Island must present valid identification, such as a current driver's license, at the time of entry. **ALL** vehicles are subject to a security search.

> **From the DGIF website:** The **Virginia Department of Game and Inland Fisheries (DGIF)** will require an **Access Permit** for visitors to department-owned Wildlife Management Areas (WMAs) and public fishing lakes **effective January 1, 2012**, who are age 17 and older, unless they possess a valid Virginia hunting, freshwater fishing, or trapping license, or a current Virginia boat registration, or are otherwise waived.

### Chippokes Plantation State Park

This is destination **CTW05** on the Virginia Birding and Wildlife Trail. The park is located off Route 634 in Surry County. It encompasses 1,683 acres of rural farmland and is bounded on the northeast by the James River.

# References

The references listed below served as primary resources for preparation of this document, and are by no means to be considered a complete and exhaustive bibliography of avian or land use information for Virginia's Colonial Historic Triangle.

Adams, M. T. and M. Hafner. 2009. Middle Atlantic. North American Birds 62(4): 541–544.

Adams, M. T. and M. Hafner. 2009. Middle Atlantic. North American Birds 63(1): 54–60.

Adams, M. T. and M. Hafner. 2009. Middle Atlantic. North American Birds 63(2): 237–241.

Adams, M. T. and M. Hafner. 2009. Middle Atlantic. North American Birds 63(3): 403–406.

Adams, M. T. and M. Hafner. 2010. Middle Atlantic. North American Birds 63(4): 578–581.

Adams, M. T. and M. Hafner. 2010. Middle Atlantic. North American Birds 64(1): 50–54.

Adams, M. T. and M. Hafner. 2010. Middle Atlantic. North American Birds 64(2): 237–240.

Adams, M. T. and M. Hafner. 2010. Middle Atlantic. North American Birds 64(3): 402–405.

Adams, M. T. and M. Hafner. 2011. Middle Atlantic. North American Birds 64(4): 575–577.

Adams, M. T. and M. Hafner. 2011. Middle Atlantic. North American Birds 65(1): 50–55.

Adams, M. T. and M. Hafner. 2011. Middle Atlantic. North American Birds 65(2): 249–253.

Adams, M. T. and M. Hafner. 2011. Middle Atlantic. North American Birds 65(3): 419–422.

Adams, M. T., M. Hafner, and R. Ostrowski. 2012. Middle Atlantic. North American Birds 65(4): 604–607.

Ake, R. A. and F. R. Scott. 1976. News and Notes: 1974 summer and fall shorebird highlights. Raven 47(2): 46–47.

Ake, R. A. and F. R. Scott. 1976. News and Notes: late cuckoo and hummingbird. Raven 47(2): 48.

Ake, R. A. and F. R. Scott. 1976. News and Notes: Spotted Sandpipers in winter. Raven 47(4): 76.

American Ornithologists' Union. 1985. Thirty-fifth supplement to the American Ornithologists' Union check-list of North American birds. Auk 102: 680–686.

Anonymous. 1969. Foreign recovery information exchange. EBBA News 32(5): 240.

Armistead, H. T. 1983. Middle Atlantic Coast Region. American Birds 37(2): 164–167.

Armistead, H. T. 1983. Middle Atlantic Coast Region. American Birds 37(3): 288–292.

Armistead, H. T. 1983. Middle Atlantic Coast Region. American Birds 37(6): 975–977.

Armistead, H. A. 1984. Middle Atlantic Coast Region. American Birds 38: 302–305.

Armistead, H. T. 1991. Middle Atlantic Coast Region. American Birds 45(5): 1101–1106.

Armour, T. C. 1980. Magnificent Frigatebird on James River. Raven 51(3): 54.

Bailey, H. H. 1913. The Birds of Virginia. J. P. Bell Co, Lynchburg.

Bailey, H. H. 1927. Data concerning the breeding range of certain marsh birds. Wilson Bull. 39: 175–177.

Barber, M. 1976. The vertebrate fauna from a late eighteenth century well: the Bray Plantation, Kingsmill, Virginia. Virginia Archaeology 10: 68–72.

Beasley, R. J. 1947. Winter birds of the York-James River Peninsula. Raven 18(5 & 6): 31–32.

Beasley, R. J. 1947. Spring birding in the Yorktown-Newport News area. Raven (9 & 10): 47–48.

Beatty, R. C. and W. J. Mulloy. 1940. William Byrd's Natural History of Virginia. Dietz Press, Richmond, Virginia.

Beck, R. 1988. Colonial Bird Investigations Study No. VI: Virginia Nongame and Endangered Wildlife Investigations: Unpublished Annual Report July 1, 1987–June 30, 1988. Virginia Department of Game and Inland Fisheries.

Blem, C. 1973. White-fronted Geese at Hog Island Refuge. Raven 44(4): 96.

Bowen, J. 1996. Foodways in the 18th-century Chesapeake. In: The archaeology of 18th-century Virginia. T. R. Reinhart, ed. Special Publ. 35 Archaeological Society of Virginia.

Bowen, J. and S. T. Andrews. 2000. The starving time at Jamestown: faunal analysis of Pit 1, Pit 3, the Bulwark Ditch, Ditch 6, Ditch 7, and Midden 1, James City County, Virginia. Report submitted to William Kelso, Jamestown Rediscovery, Association for the Preservation of Virginia Antiquities.

Bradshaw, D. 1996. Tree Sparrow invasion. Cornerstone: a publication of the Center for Conservation Biology, College of William and Mary. 2(1): 25.

Bradshaw, D.S. 1999. Faunal survey of the Green Spring Unit of Colonial National Historical Park. Center for Conservation Biology Technical Report Series, CCBTR-99-05. College of William and Mary, Williamsburg, VA. 24 pp.

Bradshaw, D. S. and B. D. Watts. 1998. Status of breeding Bald Eagles and Great Blue Herons within Colonial National Historical Park. Bald Eagle / Heron Survey Report for Colonial National Historical Park. Center for Conservation Biology Technical Report Series, CCBTR-98-05. College of William and Mary, Williamsburg, VA. 16 pp.

Breeding, R. 1993. Avifauna monitoring program implementation in the Chesapeake Bay National Estuarine Research Reserve System in Virginia: Phase One. Final report submitted to Sanctuaries and Research Division, National Oceanic and Atmospheric Administration, Chesapeake Bay National Estuarine Research Reserve System, Virginia Institute of Marine Science, Gloucester Point, VA. 86 pp.

Brinkley, E. S., C. M. Stinson, B. Taber, and B. Williams. 2001. Seabird records associated with hurricane activity in Virginia in the late 1990s. Raven 72(2): 95–125.

Brinkley, E. S. 2001. Spotted Towhee (Pipilo maculatus) at Barlow Pond, York and James City Counties. Raven 72(2): 159–161.

Brinkley, E. S. 2007. National Wildlife Federation Field Guide to Birds of North America. Sterling Publishing Company, Inc., New York.

Brinkley, E. S. 2008. Middle Atlantic. North American Birds 62(3): 385–390.

Brinkley, E. S. and G. L. Armistead. 2003. LeConte's Sparrows (*Ammodramus leconti*) in Virginia: a review of records, with notes on habitat usage, identification, and interspecific associations. Raven 74(2): 13–24.

Brown, J. and S. Erdle. 2009. Amphibians, reptiles, birds and mammals of the York River. In: Moore, K.A. and W.G. Reay. 2009. A Site Profile of the Chesapeake Bay National Estuarine Research Reserve in Virginia. Virginia Institute of Marine Science, College of William and Mary. Gloucester Point, VA.

Buckley, Neil J. 1999. Black Vulture (*Coragyps atratus*), The Birds of North America Online (A. Poole, Ed.). Ithaca: Cornell Lab of Ornithology. Retrieved from the Birds of North America Online at http://bna.birds.cornell.edu/bna/species/411.

Byrd, M. A. 1966. A record of the Northern Shrike in southeastern Virginia. Raven 37(3): 63.

Byrd, M. 1969. The 1969 VSO annual meeting. Raven 40(2): 38–41.

Byrd, M. 1972. North American Osprey Research Conference. Raven 43(2): 23–26.

Byrd, M. A., B. Akers, J. Via, and B. Williams. 1974. Avifauna of the VEPCO Surry Nuclear Power Plant. In: Study of the vascular flora and terrestrial fauna of the Surry Nuclear Plant Area, Surry County, Virginia. M. A. Byrd, G.R. Brooks, D Ware, S. Ware, and J. Via eds. Department of Biology College of William and Mary, Williamsburg, Virginia, pp 81–129.

Byrd, M. A., R. Cashwell, and K. Terwilliger. 1987. Peregrine Falcon investigations. Virginia nongame and endangered wildlife investigations: Annual Report July 1, 1986–June 30, 1987. Virginia Department of Game and Inland Fisheries, Richmond. pp. 38–41.

Byrd, M. A., R. Cashwell, and K. Terwilliger. 1988. Peregrine Falcon investigations. Virginia nongame and endangered wildlife investigations: Annual Report July 1, 1987–June 30, 1988. Virginia Department of Game and Inland Fisheries, Richmond. pp. 54–74.

Byrd, M. A., R. Cashwell, K. Terwilliger and A. Wheely. 1989. Peregrine Falcon investigations. Virginia nongame and endangered species investigations: Annual Report July 1, 1988–June 30, 1989. Virginia Department of Game and Inland Fisheries, Richmond. pp. 47–49.

Byrd, M. A., K. Terwilliger, R. Beck, B. Watts, and D. Bradshaw. 1986. Colonial bird investigations. Virginia nongame and endangered wildlife investigations: Annual Report July 1, 1986–June 30, 1987. Virginia Department of Game and Inland Fisheries, Richmond. pp. 47–62.

Byrd, M. A., K. Terwilliger, D. Bradshaw, and R. Reynolds. 1992. Peregrine Falcon investigations. Wildlife Division Annual Report: Nongame and Endangered Species Program. July 1, 1991–June 30, 1992. Virginia Department of Game and Inland Fisheries, Richmond. pp. 29–32.

Chesser, R. T., R. C. Banks, F. K. Barker, C. Cicero, J. L. Dunn, A. W. Krattter, I. J. Lovette, P. C. Rasmussen, J. V. Remson, J. D. Rising, D. F. Stotz, and K. Winker. 2009. Fiftieth supplement to the American Ornithologists' Union Check-list of North American Birds. Auk 126(3): 726–744.

Chesser, R. T., R. C. Banks, F. K. Barker, C. Cicero, J. L. Dunn, A. W. Kratter, I. J. Lovette, P. C. Rasmussen, J. V. Remson, J. D. Rising, D. F. Stotz, and K. Winker. 2010.

Fifty-first supplement to the American Ornithologists' Union Check-list of North American Birds. Auk 127(3): 705–714.

Chesser, R. T., R. C. Banks, F. K. Barker, C. Cicero, J. L. Dunn, A. W. Kratter, I. J. Lovette, P. C. Rasmussen, J. V. Remson, J. D. Rising, D. F. Stotz, and K. Winker. 2011. Fifty-second supplement to the American Ornithologists' Union Check-list of North American Birds. Auk 128(3): 600–613.

Chesser, R. T., R. C. Banks, F. K. Barker, C. Cicero, J. L. Dunn, A. W. Kratter, I. J. Lovette, P. C. Rasmussen, J. V. Remson, J. D. Rising, D. F. Stotz, and K. Winker. 2012. Fifty-third supplement to the American Ornithologists' Union Check-list of North American Birds. Auk 129(3): 573–588.

Chickahominy River Recreational Access Study-Richmond Regional Planning District Commission October 31, 2007.

City of Williamsburg, Virginia's Colonial Capital: Comprehensive Plan. Adopted October 12, 2006.

Clapp, R. B. 1986. A Black-headed Grosbeak specimen from Virginia. Raven: 1–3.

Clapp, R. B. 1997. Egg dates for Virginia birds. Virginia Avifauna No. 6, Virginia Society of Ornithology.

Clark, H. C. 1938. Notes on Virginia birds. Raven 9(4 & 5): 29–31.

Craig, J. 1955. Trip to Hog Island. Raven 26(4): 59.

Craven, A. O. 1965. Soil exhaustion as a factor in the agricultural history of Virginia and Maryland, 1606–1860. University of Illinois Press.

Cross, B. 1999. 1998 report of the Virginia Avian Records Committee. Raven 70(1): 26–32.

Cross, B. 2000. 1999 report of the Virginia Avian Records Committee. Raven 71(1): 25–29.

Crowder, O. B. 1976. Foraging ecology of the Common Yellowthroat, the Prairie, Warbler, and the White-eyed Vireo. M. A. thesis, College of William and Mary, Williamsburg, VA.

Dalmas, T. 1993. White Ibises at Hog Island Wildlife Management Area. Raven 64(2): 87.

Daniel, B. 1952. A visit to Virginia Beach, Jamestown, and Cape Charles. Raven 23(7 & 8): 69–70.

Dauphine, D. 1687. A Huguenot exile in Virginia; being the memoirs of a Huguenot refugee in 1686. Translated by a Virginian, Fairfax Harrison, 1923, Richmond.

Davis, A. 2012. Sightings: mid-November to mid-December 2011. Birding 44(1): 18–21.

Davis, B. 1986. Faunal analysis at Governor's Land; two rural eighteenth century sites in James City County, Virginia. M. A. thesis, Hunter College, CUNY.

Day, T. M. 2007. Middle Atlantic. North American Birds. 60(4): 513–516.

Devan, S. 2009. Townsend's Solitaire in James City County, January–April 2008. Raven 80(1 & 2): 3–4.

Dolby, A. 2007. The 2007 state park breeding bird foray. Raven 78(2): 27–38.

D'Onofrio, A. 2004. Fall records Aug–Nov 2004. Southeast Region. Virginia Birds 1(2): 17–19.

D'Onofrio, A. 2005. Winter records Dec 2004–Feb 2005. Southeast Region. Virginia Birds 1(3): 16–17.

D'Onofrio, A. 2005. Spring records Mar–May 2005. Southeast Region. Virginia Birds 1(4): 19–21.

D'Onofrio, A. 2005. Summer records June–July 2005. Southeast Region. Virginia Birds 2(1): 17–19.

D'Onofrio, A. 2005. Fall records August–November 2005. Southeast Region. Virginia Birds 2(2): 18–20.

D'Onofrio, A. 2006. Winter records December 2005–February 2006. Southeast Region. Virginia Birds 2(3): 12–14.

D'Onofrio, A. 2006. Spring records March 2006–May 2006. Southeast Region. Virginia Birds 2(4): 15–17.

D'Onofrio, A. 2006. Summer records June 2006–July 2006. Southeast Region. Virginia Birds 3(1): 8–9.

D'Onofrio, A. 2006. Fall records August 2006–November 2006. Southeast Region. Virginia Birds 3(2): 14–16.

D'Onofrio, A. 2007. Winter records December 2006–February 2007. Southeast Region. Virginia Birds 3(3): 25–26.

D'Onofrio, A. 2007. Spring records March 2007–May 2007. Southeast Region. Virginia Birds 3(4): 8–9.

D'Onofrio, A. 2007. Summer records June 2007–July 2007. Southeast Region. Virginia Birds 4(1): 6–7.

D'Onofrio, A. 2007. Fall Records August 2007–November 2007. Southeast Region. Virginia Birds 4(2): 12–14.

D'Onofrio, A. 2008. Winter records December 2007–February 2008. Southeast Region. Virginia Birds 4(3): 8–9.

D'Onofrio, A. 2008. Spring records March 2008–May 2008. Southeast Region. Virginia Birds 4(4): 12–13.

D'Onofrio, A. 2008. Summer records June 2008–July 2008. Southeast Region. Virginia Birds 5(1): 6–7.

D'Onofrio, A. 2008. Fall records August 2008–November 2008. Southeast Region. Virginia Birds 5(2): 15–17.

D'Onofrio, A. 2009. Winter records December 2008–February 2009. Southeast Region. Virginia Birds 5(3): 11–13.

D'Onofrio, A. 2009. Spring records March–May 2009. Southeast Region. Virginia Birds 5(4): 17–20.

D'Onofrio, A. 2009. Summer records June–July 2009. Southeast Region. Virginia Birds 6(1): 9–10.

D'Onofrio, A. 2009. Fall records August–November 2009. Southeast Region. Virginia Birds 6(2): 12–13.

D'Onofrio, A. 201. Winter records December 2009–February 2010. Southeast Region. Virginia Birds 6(3): 11–12.

D'Onofrio, A. 2010. Spring records March–May 2010. Southeast Region. Virginia Birds 6(4): 8–9.

D'Onofrio, A. 2010. Summer records June–July 2010. Southeast Region. Virginia Birds 7(1): 8–9.

D'Onofrio, A. 2010. Fall records August–November 2010. Southeast Region. Virginia Birds 7(2): 14–16.

D'Onofrio, A. 2011. Winter records December 2010–February 2011. Southeast Region. Virginia Birds 7(3): 16–17.

D'Onofrio, A. 2011. Spring records March 2011–May 2011. Southeast Region. Virginia Birds 7(4): 15–17. [published as 7(3)].

Dunn, J. L. and J. Alderfer. 2006. National Geographic Field Guide to the Birds of North America. Fifth Edition. National Geographic Society, Washington, D. C.

Ealding, W. 2011. Annual report of the Virginia Avian Records Committee. Raven 81(2): 21–22.

eBird. 2012. eBird: An online database of bird distribution and abundance [web application]. Version 2 eBird, Ithaca, New York. Available at http://www.ebird.org. (Accessed: 23 Jun 2012).

Erdle, S. Y. and K. E. Heffernan. 2005. Management Plan for Goodwin Islands: Chesapeake Bay National Estuarine Research Reserve -Virginia. Natural Heritage Technical Report #05–03. Virginia Department of Conservation and Recreation, Division of Natural Heritage. Richmond, Virginia. 46 pp. plus appendices.

Feduccia, A. 1989. Birds of Colonial Williamsburg: A historical portfolio. The Colonial Williamsburg Foundation, Williamsburg, VA.

Fleming, G. P. and K. D. Patterson. 2012. Natural Communities of Virginia: Ecological Groups and Community Types. Natural Heritage Technical Report 12-04. Virginia Department of Conservation and Recreation, Division of Natural Heritage, Richmond, Virginia. 36 pages.

Fleming, G.P., K.D. Patterson, K. Taverna, and P.P. Coulling. 2012. The natural communities of Virginia: classification of ecological community groups. Second approximation. Version 2.5. Virginia Department of Conservation and Recreation, Division of Natural Heritage, Richmond, VA.

Frost, C. 1993. Four centuries of changing landscape patterns in the longleaf pine ecosystem. Proceedings of the Tall Timbers Fire Ecology Conference, No 18, The Longleaf Pine Ecosystem: ecology and management. S. M. Hermann, ed. Tall Timbers Reaserch Station, Tallahassee, FL.

Gilmer, A. 2010. Annual report of the Virginia Avian Records Committee. Raven 81(1): 30–33.

Grey, J. H. 1954. Twenty-five years of Christmas bird counts in Virginia. Raven 25(1): 5–8.

Grey, J. H. 1954. Summary of 1953 Christmas Bird Counts in Virginia. Raven 25(1): 20–23.

Grey, J. H. 1955. Summary of 1954 Christmas bird counts in Virginia. Raven 26(1): 26–29.

Grey, J. H. 1960. Fulvous Tree Ducks at Williamsburg, Virginia. Raven 31(11 & 12): 104–105.

Hague, F. S. 1952. Nineteenth annual meeting. Raven 23(3 & 4): 17–19.

Hague, F. S. 1952. Annual meeting field trip. Raven 23(3 & 4): 19.

Haile, E. W. 1998. Jamestown Narratives: eyewitness accounts of the Virginia Colony, the first decade, 1607–1617. Roundhouse, Champlain, Virginia.

Haramis, G. M. and G. D. Kearns. 2007. Soras in tidal marsh: banding and telemetry studies on the Patuxent River, Maryland. Waterbirds 30 (Special Publication 1): 105–121.

Harriot, T. 1590. [1972]. A briefe and true report of the new found land of Virginia. Dover, New York.

Heath, S. A. 2007. 2006 annual report of the Virginia Avian Records Committee. Raven 78(1): 57–62.

Historic Past, Sustainable Future. 2009 James City County Comprehensive Plan. Adopted 24 November 2009.

Horn, J. 2005. A land as God made it: Jamestown and the birth of America. Basic Books, New York.

Howell, S. N. G. and J. Dunn. 2007. Gulls of the Americas. Houghton Mifflin Company, New York.

Hume, I. N. 1963. Here lies Virginia. Alfred Knopf, New York.

Johnston, D. W. (comp). 1999. A Birder's Guide to Virginia. American Birding Association, Colorado Springs, CO.

Johnston, D. W. 2003. The History of Ornithology in Virginia. University of Virginia Press, Charlottesville, Virginia.

Jones, F. M. Unpublished field notes of Virginia egg collections.

Kain, T. 1984. Virginia Christmas bird counts: 1983–84 season. Raven 55[54]: 17–29.

Kain, T. 1985. Virginia Christmas bird counts: 1984–85 season. Raven 56: 4–19.

Kain, T. 1986. Virginia Christmas bird counts: 1985–86 season. Raven 57: 39–63.

Kain, T. 1987. Virginia Christmas bird counts: 1986–87 season. Raven 58: 37–61.

Kain, T. 1987. Virginia's Birdlife: an annotated checklist. Virginia Avifauna No. 3, Virginia Society of Ornithology.

Kain, T. 1988. Virginia Christmas bird counts: 1987–88 season. Raven 59: 39–64.

Kain, T. 1990. Virginia Christmas bird counts: 1988–89 season. Raven 61(1): 17–43.

Kain, T. 1991. Virginia Christmas bird counts: 1989–90 season. Raven 62(1): 15–40.

Kain, T. 1992. Virginia Christmas bird counts: 1990–91 season. Raven 63(1): 35–62.

Kain, T. 1993. Virginia Christmas bird counts: 1991–92 season. Raven 64(1): 34–62.

Kain, T. 1994. Virginia Christmas bird counts: 1992–93 season. Raven 65(1): 45–71.

Kain, T. 1995. Virginia Christmas bird counts: 1993–94 season. Raven 66(1): 45–75.

Kain, T. 1996. Virginia Christmas bird counts: 1994–95 season. Raven 67(1): 37–72.

Kain, T. 1997. Virginia Christmas bird counts: 1995–1996. Raven 68(1): 49–81.

Kain, T. 1997. Virginia Christmas bird counts: 1996–97 season. Raven 68(2): 119–155.

Kain, T. 1998. Virginia Christmas bird counts: 1997–98 season. Raven 69(2): 76–109.

Kain, T. 1999. Virginia Christmas bird counts: 1998–99 season. Raven 70(2): 53–86.

Kain, T. 2000. Virginia Christmas bird counts: 1999–2000 season. Raven 71(2): 71–104.

Kain, T. 2001. Virginia Christmas bird counts: 2000–2001 season. Raven 72(1): 17–51.

Kain, T. 2002. Virginia Christmas bird counts: 2001–2002 season. Raven 73(1): 17–54.

Kain, T. 2003. Virginia Christmas bird counts: 2002–2003 season. Raven 74(1): 18–63.

Kain, T. 2004. Virginia Christmas bird counts: 2003–2004 season. Raven 75(1): 16–60.

Kain, T. 2005. Virginia Christmas bird counts: 2004–2005 season. Raven 76(1): 22–66.

Kain, T. 2006. Virginia Christmas bird counts: 2005–2006 season. Raven 77(1): 16–49.

Kain, T. 2007. Virginia Christmas bird counts: 2004–2005 season. Raven 78(1): 15–49.

Kain, T. 2008. Virginia Christmas bird counts: 2007–2008 season. Raven 79(1 & 2): 8–36. Raven 80 (1 & 2): 52–54.

Kain, T. 2009. Virginia Christmas Bird Counts: 2008–2009 season. Raven 80(1 & 2): 29–45.

Kain, T. 2010. The 110th Christmas Bird Count: Washington, DC/Virginia. American Birds 64: 48–49.

Kain, T. 2010. Virginia Christmas Bird Counts: 2009–2010 season. Raven 81(1): 8–21.

Kain, T. 2011. Virginia Christmas Bird Counts: 2010–2011 season. Raven 81(2): 3–20.

Kain, T. 2012. Virginia Christmas Bird Counts: 2011–2012 season. Raven 83(1): 3–31.

Kennedy, R. S. 1971. Population dynamics of Ospreys in Tidewater, Virginia, 1970–1971. M. A. thesis, College of William and Mary, Williamsburg, VA.

Laing, W. N. 1959. Cattle in 17th century Virginia. Virginia Magazine of History and Biography 67(2): 143–163.

Langley, C. 2009. Rare gull lands near ferry friends. The Virginia Gazette. Mid-week Edition, July 1, 2009 pg. 8A.

Larner, Y. 1979. Virginia's Birdlife: an annotated checklist. Virginia Avifauna No. 2, Virginia Society of Ornithology.

Larner, Y. and F. R. Scott. 1979. News and Notes: Redpoll invasion. Raven 50(2): 40.

Larner, Y. and F. R. Scott. 1979. News and Notes: Upland Sandpipers in spring and summer. Raven 50(3): 63.

Larner, Y. and F. R. Scott. 1981. News and Notes: Sooty Terns in Virginia. Raven 52(1): 16.

Larner, Y. and F. R. Scott. 1982. News and Notes: migrating swans in York County. Raven 53(2): 40.

Larner, Y. and F. R. Scott. 1983. News and Notes: White-fronted Geese in winter. Raven 54(1): 21–22.

Lawson, J. [1709]. A new voyage to Carolina ... Edited by Hugh T. Lefler, University of North Carolina Press, Chapel Hill, N.C. 1967.

LeClerc, J. E. 2002. The 2002 golf course foray. Raven 73(2): 3–43.

Lewis, S. 2009. Images of America: James City County. Arcadia Publishing, Mount Pleasant, S.C.

Ludwig, J. C., K. A. Buhlman, and C. A. Pague. 1993. A Natural Heritage inventory of Mid-Atlantic Region National Parks in Virginia: Colonial National Historic Park. Natural Heritage Technical Report #93-6, Virginia Department of Conservation and Recreation Division of Natural Heritage, Richmond, Virginia.

Mackenzie, L. L. 1944. A Mallard's nest in Princess Anne County, Virginia. Raven 15(6): 48.

Mann, C. C. 2005. 1491: new revelations of the Americas before Columbus. Vintage, New York.

Manning-Sterling, E. 1994. Great Blue Herons and River Otters: the changing perceptions of all things wild in the seventeenth and eighteenth-century Chesapeake. M.A. thesis, College of William and Mary, Williamsburg, VA.

McBurney, H. 1997. Mark Catesby's natural history of America: the watercolors from the Royal Library Windsor Castle. Merrell Holberton, London.

McCartney, M. C. 1997. James City County: Keystone of the Commonwealth. The Donning Co., Virginia Beach, VA.

McClain, J. 2010. Cracking the case: William and Mary faculty and students team up to solve the mystery of the Rusty Blackbirds. William and Mary Alumni Magazine 75(4): 44–47.

McClain, J. 2010. Raptors nest above Sunken Garden. William and Mary News and Events: 2 April 2010 at http://www.wm.edu/news/stories/2010/hawks-007.php.

McKinley, D. 1979. The Carolina Parakeet in the Virginias: a review. Raven 49(1): 3–10.

Meanley, B. 1975. Birds and marshes of the Chesapeake Bay country. Tidewater Publishers, Cambridge, MD.

Molineux, W. 2001. Images of America: Williamsburg. Arcadia Publishing, Mount Pleasant, S.C.

Murray, J. J. 1931. Field Notes. Raven 2(4): 4–7.

Murray, J. J. 1947. The 1946 Christmas bird census. Raven 18(1 & 2): 4–9.

Murray, J. J. 1948. The 1947 Christmas bird census. Raven 19(1 & 2): 7–11.

Murray, J. J. 1949. The 1948 Christmas Bird Census. Raven 20(1 & 2): 7–14.

Murray, J. J. 1949. Spring season-1949-Virginia. Raven 20(7 & 8): 50–53.

Murray, J. J. 1949. Summer Season-1949-Virginia. Raven 20(9 & 10): 62–65.

Murray, J. J. 1950. The Christmas Census-1949-Virginia. Raven 21 (1 & 2): 4–13.

Murray, J. J. 1950. Notes and News. Raven 21(3 & 4): 17–18.

Murray, J. J. 1951. Christmas Counts-1950-Virginia. Raven 22(1 & 2): 2–10.

Murray, J. J. 1952. A check-list of the birds of Virginia. Virginia Society of Ornithology.

Murray, J. J. 1952. Virginia Christmas counts-1951. Raven 23(1 & 2): 2–9.

Murray, J. J. 1952. Gaps in our knowledge of Virginia birds. Raven 23(11 & 12): 94–96.

Murray, J. J. 1953. First revision of the Virginia 1952 'checklist'. Raven 24(5 & 6): 34–46.

Murray, J. J. 1953. Virginia Christmas Bird Counts-1952. Raven 24(1 & 2): 7–16.

Murray, J. J. 1954. Virginia Christmas Bird Counts. Raven 25(1): 8–20.

Murray, J. J. 1954. Virginia bird notes. Raven 25(5 & 6): 88–89.

Murray, J. J. 1954. Virginia bird notes. Raven 25(7 & 8): 104–105.

Murray, J. J. 1955. Virginia Christmas bird counts-1954. Raven 26(1): 12–26.

Murray, J. J. 1955. News and Notes. Raven 26(2 & 3): 48–49.

Murray, J. J. 1955. Second revision of the Virginia 1952 'checklist'. Raven 26(6 & 7): 75–97.

Murray, J. J. 1956. Virginia Christmas bird counts-1955. Raven 27(1 & 2): 2–15.

Murray, J. J. 1956. Virginia Notes. Raven 27(5 & 6): 44–46.

Murray, J. J. 1957. Virginia Christmas bird counts-1956. Raven 28(1 & 2): 7–18.

Murray, J. J. 1957. Major recent changes in the Virginia avifauna. Raven 28(5 & 6): 48–52.

Murray, J. J. 1959. Virginia Christmas bird counts, 1958-1959. Raven 30(1 & 2): 3–15.

Murray, J. J. 1960. Virginia Christmas bird counts, 1959-1960. Raven 31(1 & 2): 5–18.

Murray, J. J. 1960. News and Notes: Western Kingbird. Raven 31(11 & 12): 113–115.

Murray, J. J. 1961. News and Notes: Cattle Egrets inland in Virginia. Raven 32(5 & 6): 76–77.

Murray, J. J. 1962. News and Notes. Raven 33(2): 14–16.

Murray, J. J. 1963. Spread of the Cattle Egret in Virginia. Raven 34(1): 17–18.

Murray, J. J. 1963. News and Notes. Raven 34(1): 23–24.

Murray, J. J. 1963. Fourth revision of the 1952 Virginia 'checklist'. Raven 34(2): 27–28.

Murray, J. J. 1963. News and Notes. Raven 34(3): 45–47.

Murray, J. J. 1965. News and Notes: Fulvous Tree Ducks in Virginia. Raven 36(1): 27–2.

Murray, J. J. 1968. News and Notes: Boat-tailed Grackles nesting inland. Raven 39(4): 73–74.

Murray, J. J. 1969. News and Notes: Common Egrets inland in winter. Raven 40(2): 44.

Murray, J. J. and R. O. Paxton. 1962. Southward dispersal into Virginia of the Evening Grosbeak. Raven 33(2): 7–10.

Myers, R.K., K.E. Heffernan, P.P. Coulling, A. Belden, and A.C. Chazal. 2008. Management Plan for Taskinas Creek Chesapeake Bay National Estuarine Research Reserve. Natural Heritage Technical Report #07-10. Virginia Department of Conservation and Recreation, Division of Natural Heritage. Richmond, Virginia. 43 pages plus appendices.

Nicholson, F. 1698. Francis Nicholson Papers, 1680–1721: folder 2, document 6-Virginia_James City, March ye 1st 1698 (9).

Oakes, M. 1968. Ten years of banding Purple Finches at Westpoint, Mass. EBBA News 31(2): 73–74.

Paxton, B. J. 2006. Potential Impact of Common Reed Expansion on Threatened Highmarsh Bird Communities on the Seaside: Assessment of Phragmites Invasion of High Marsh Habitats. Center for Conservation Biology Technical Report Series, CCBTR-06-17. College of William and Mary, Williamsburg, VA. 9 pp.

Paxton, R. O. 1952. The Evening Grosbeak invasion, 1951–52, in Virginia. Raven 23(7 & 8): 58–62.

Paxton, R. O. 1959. The Evening Grosbeak in Virginia 1957–1958. Raven 29(5 & 6): 49–53.

Potter, J. and J. J. Murray. 1954. Middle Atlantic Coast Region. Winter Season. Audubon Field Notes 8: 244.

Ridd, S. 1987. 1987 Breeding Bird Atlas Project results. Raven 58: 71–73.

Rives, W. C. 1890. A catalogue of the birds of the Virginias. Proceedings of the Newport Natural History Society, 1889–1890, Document VII, Newport, Rhode Island.

Rottenborn, S. C. and E. S. Brinkley. 2007. Virginia's Birdlife: an annotated checklist- fourth edition. Virginia Avifauna No. 7, Virginia Society of Ornithology.

Scott, F. R. 1947. Chesapeake Bay Notes. Raven 18(1 & 2): 3–4.

Scott, F. R. 1948. A trip down the Chickahominy. Raven 19(7 & 8): 42–44.

Scott, F. R. 1949. Random notes. Raven 20(5 & 6): 36–37.

Scott, F. R. 1950. Winter season-1949-1950-Virginia. Raven 21(11 & 12): 100–101.

Scott, F. R. 1951. Spring season-1950-Virginia Raven 22(1 & 2): 10–13.

Scott, F. R. 1951. Nesting season-1950-Virginia. Raven 22(5 & 6): 29–30.

Scott, F. R. 1951. Fall season-1950-Virginia. Raven 22(5 & 6): 30–32.

Scott, F. R. 1951. Winter season-1950-1951-Virginia. Raven 22(7 & 8): 42–43.

Scott, F. R. 1952. The Spring season in Virginia-1951. Raven 23(3 & 4): 20–22.

Scott, F. R. 1952. The 1951 fall migration in Virginia. Raven 23(11 & 12): 96–98.

Scott, F. R. 1952. The 1951-1952 winter season in Virginia. Raven 23 (11 & 12): 98–100.

Scott, F. R. 1953. The 1952 spring season in Virginia. Raven 24(3 & 4): 25–27.

Scott, F. R. 1953. The 1952 nesting season in Virginia. Raven 24(5 & 6): 52–53.

Scott, F. R. 1953. The 1952 fall migration season. Raven 24(7 & 8): 64–67.

Scott, F. R. 1953. The 1952-1953 winter season in Virginia. Raven 24(9 & 10): 71–73.

Scott, F. R. 1954. The 1953 spring migration in Virginia. Raven 25(2 & 3): 26–28.

Scott, F. R. 1954. The 1953 summer season in Virginia. Raven 25(7 & 8): 97–99.

Scott, F. R. 1954. The 1953 fall migration in Virginia. Raven 25(11): 135–138.

Scott, F. R. 1955. Virginia season reports: winter-1953-1954. Raven 26(12): 123–125.

Scott, F. R. 1955. Virginia season report: the 1954 spring migration. Raven 26(12): 125–126.

Scott, F. R. 1955. Virginia season report: the 1954 summer season. Raven 26(12): 126–128.

Scott, F. R. 1955. Virginia season report: the 1954 fall migration. Raven 26(12): 128–130.

Scott, F. R. 1956. Least Terns nesting on lower James River. Raven 27 (5, 6, & 7): 54.

Scott, F. R. 1959. Middle Atlantic Coast Region. Audubon Field Notes 13(4): 358–360.

Scott, F. R. 1960. The 1959-1960 Christmas bird counts in Virginia. Raven 31(1 & 2): 2–5.

Scott, F. R. 1963. The Bald Eagle survey in Virginia-interim status report. Raven 34(1): 18–21.

Scott, F. R. 1964. Some northern birds in Virginia-winter 1963–64. Raven 35(3): 41–43.

Scott, F. R. 1964. Notes on heronries in Central Virginia. Raven 35(3): 46.

Scott, F. R. 1964. Sight record of a Western Grebe. Raven 35(3): 46–47.

Scott, F. R. 1969. News and Notes: Lincoln's Sparrow in spring. Raven 40(3): 57–60.

Scott, F. R. 1969. News and Notes: White Ibis appear again. Raven 40(4): 82–83.

Scott, F. R. 1970. News and Notes: Early warbler transients. Raven 41(2): 39–40.

Scott, F. R. 1970. News and Notes: European Widgeon influx. Raven 41(3): 53–55.

Scott, F. R. 1970. Northern finches again invade Virginia. Raven 41(4): 63–65.

Scott, F. R. 1971. News and Notes: White Ibis again invade Virginia. Raven 42(2): 38.

Scott, F. R. 1971. News and Notes: unusual warblers in Williamsburg. Raven 42(2): 41.

Scott, F. R. 1971. News and Notes: winter and early arriving Ospreys. Raven 42(3): 54.

Scott, F. R. 1971. News and Notes: winter Whimbrel inland. Raven 42(3): 55.

Scott, F. R. 1971. News and Notes: recent unusual gulls and terns. Raven42(4): 69.

Scott, F. R. 1974. News and Notes: Buff-breasts recorded. Raven 45(1): 31.

Scott, F. R. 1975. News and Notes: Bonaparte's Gulls in summer. Raven 46(2): 56.

Scott, F. R. 1975. News and Notes: Caspian Terns in summer. Raven 46(3): 71.

Scott, F. R. 1975. News and Notes: Bobolinks in summer. Raven 46(3): 72.

Scott, F. R. 1976. News and Notes: White Ibis in 1974. Raven 47(1): 29.

Scott, F. R. 1976. News and Notes: Mourning Warblers in eastern Virginia. Raven 47(1): 31.

Scott, F. R. 1977. News and Notes: Wood Stork in Surry County. Raven 48(1): 32.

Scott, F. R. 1978. News and Notes: Tree Swallow nesting near Williamsburg. Raven 49(1): 15.

Scott, F. R. 1978. Virginia Christmas bird counts-1977-1978 season. Raven 49(2): 19–32.

Scott, F. R. 1979. Virginia Christmas bird counts-1978-1979 season. Raven 50(2): 19–33.

Scott, F. R. 1979. Middle Atlantic Coast Region. American Birds 33(5): 758–760.

Scott, F. R. 1980. Virginia Christmas bird counts-1979-80 season. Raven 51(2): 19–33.

Scott, F. R. 1981. Virginia Christmas bird counts-1980-81 season. Raven 52(2): 19–33.

Scott, F. R. 1982. Virginia Christmas bird counts 1981-82 season. Raven 53(2): 19–33.

Scott, F. R. 1983. Virginia Christmas bird counts 1982-83 season. Raven 54(2): 27–42.

Scott, F. R. and D. A. Cutler. 1960. Middle Atlantic Coast Region. Audubon Field Notes 14 (5): 439–441.

Scott, F. R. and D. A. Cutler. 1961. Middle Atlantic Coast Region. Audubon Field Notes 15(1): 21.

Scott, F. R. and D. A. Cutler. 1962. Middle Atlantic Coast Region. Audubon Field Notes 16(1): 16.

Scott, F. R. and D. A. Cutler. 1963. Middle Atlantic Coast Region. Audubon Field Notes 17(4): 395.

Scott, F. R. and D. A. Cutler. 1966. Middle Atlantic Coast Region. Audubon Field Notes 20(1): 26.

Scott, F. R. and D. A. Cutler. 1966. Middle Atlantic Coast Region. Audubon Field Notes 20(5): 558.

Scott, F. R. and D. A. Cutler. 1967. Middle Atlantic Coast Region. Audubon Field Notes 21(1): 16.

Scott, F. R. and D. A. Cutler. 1967. Middle Atlantic Coast Region. Audubon Field Notes 21(4): 494.

Scott, F. R. and D. A. Cutler. 1971. Middle Atlantic Coast Region. American Birds 25(3): 558–562.

Scott, F. R. and J. K. Potter. 1959. Middle Atlantic Coast Region. Audubon Field Notes 13(5): 422–424.

Seek, G. L. 1977. The Tidewater Virginia Osprey Population: 1972 and 1973. M. A. thesis, College of William and Mary, Williamsburg, Virginia.

Sheehan, W. J. 1998. Birds of the Williamsburg Virginia area: an annotated checklist. Williamsburg Bird Club, Williamsburg, VA.

Silberhorn, G. M. 1976. Tidal wetland plants of Virginia. Educational Series no. 19. Virginia Institute of Marine Science, Gloucester Point, VA.

Smith, F.M. 2005. Summary of colonial nesting herons within the Colonial National Historic Park Boundaries, 2005. Center for Conservation Biology Technical Report Series, CCBTR-05-07. College of William and Mary, Williamsburg, VA. 13 pp.

Smith, F. M. 2006. Summary of Colonial Nesting Herons within the Colonial National Historic Park boundaries, 2006 breeding season. Center for Conservation Biology Technical Report Series, CCBTR-06-10. College of William and Mary, Williamsburg, VA, 13 pp.

Smith, F. M. 2007. Summary of colonial nesting herons within the Colonial National Historic Park boundaries, 2007 breeding season. Center for Conservation Biology Technical Report Series, CCBTR-07-05. College of William and Mary, Williamsburg, VA 13 pp.

Smith, J. 1608. A true relation of occurrences and accident of noate as hath hapned in Virginia. John Tappe, London.

Snyder, Noel F. and Keith Russell. 2002. Carolina Parakeet *(Conuropsis carolinensis)*, The Birds of North America Online (A. Poole, Ed.). Ithaca: Cornell Lab of Ornithology; Retrieved from the Birds of North America Online at http://bna.birds.cornell. edu/bna/species/667.

Steirly, C. C. 1952. King Rail nest in Surry, County, Virginia. Raven 23(7 & 8): 68–69.

Steirly, C. C. 1952. Hog Island Waterfowl Refuge. Raven 23(9 & 10): 87–89.

Steirly, C. C. 1953. Notes from Sussex and Surry Counties, Virginia. Raven 24(1 & 2): 4.

Steirly, C. C. 1953. Eastern regional trip. Raven 24(11 & 12): 89–90.

Steirly, C. C. 1956. Eastern Glossy Ibis in Surry County. Raven 27 (5 & 6): 42.

Steirly, C. C. 1958. Golden Plover in Surry County. Raven 29(1 & 2): 16.

Steirly, C. C. 1959. Breeding Clapper Rails in James River cord-grass marshes. Raven 30(3 & 4): 47–48.

Steirly, C. C. 1960. Red Phalarope in Surry County. Raven 31(5 & 6): 53.

Stierly, C. C. 1960. Defensive action of King Rail. Raven 31(9 & 10): 92.

Steirly, C. C. 1961. Bald Eagle's nest occupied by Great Horned Owl. Raven 32(7 & 8): 84.

Steirly, C. C. 1961. Fulvous Tree Duck in Surry County. Raven 32(11 & 12): 174.

Stinson, C. H. and M. A. Byrd. 1976. A comparison of past and present Osprey breeding populations in Coastal Virginia. Bird Banding 47: 258–262.

Strachey, W. 1953. The Historie of Travell into Virginia Britania. Ed. Louis B. Wright and Virginia Freund, Hakluyt Society, London, Second Series vol. 103 (initially published 1612).

Sullivan, B. and B. Taber. 2003. The status of Swainson's Hawk *(Buteo swainsoni)* in Virginia. Raven 74(1): 11–17.

Sykes, P. W. 1961. The Fulvous Tree Duck invasion into southeastern Virginia. Raven 32(5 & 6): 60–63.

Taber, B. 1992. Spring raptor migration at Williamsburg. Raven 63(2): 69–72.

Taber, B. 1997. College Creek Hawk Watch. Raven 68(2): 110–112.

Taber, B. 2000. The Turkey Vultures of College Creek. Hawk Watch Studies 25(2): 20–21.

Taber, B. 2000. Golden Eagles in late winter and spring migration near Williamsburg. Raven 71(2): 46–47.

Taber, B. 2001. Spring migration of Turkey Vultures at College Creek. Raven 72(1): 63–65.

Taber, B. 2001. Spring record of Swainson's Hawk in Virginia. Raven 72(2): 162.

Taber, B. 2002. Group water-crossing strategies in migrating Turkey Vultures. Raven 73(1): 72–74.

Taber, B. 2002. Selasphorus hummingbirds in Virginia. Raven 73(1): 66–68.

Taber, B. 2002. A six-year summary of the College Creek hawkwatch, 1997–2002. Raven 73(2): 52–54.

Taber, B. 2005. Rufous and Selasphorus hummingbirds returning to feeders in Virginia. Raven 76(1): 12–14.

Taber, B. 2007. College Creek hawk watch: a ten year summary, 1997–2006. Raven 78(1): 3–6.

Taber, B. 2007. Hummingbirds in Virginia 1 November–15 March: possible site selection criteria. Raven 78(1): 10–14.

Taber, B. and B. Williams. 1994. Williamsburg Bird Club spring counts 1978–1994: an overview summary. Raven 65(2): 90–104.

The County of York Comprehensive Plan: Charting the Course to 2025. Adopted December 6, 2005 Ordinance No. 05-35 (amended 13 & 22 May 2009; 26 March 2010)

Vaughn, S. 2011. James City County growth 5th fastest in state. Virginia Gazette. Saturday Feb. 5, 2011.

Virginia Birding and Wildlife Trail Guide. Virginia Department of Game and Inland Fisheries, Richmond, Virginia.

Virginia Gazette. 1931. White Owl Shot Near Archer's Hope. Friday edition, January 23, 1931.

Ware, S. 1970. Southern mixed hardwood forest in the Virginia Coastal Plain. Ecology Vol. 51(5): 921–924.

Ware, S., C. Frost and P D. Doerr. 1993. Southern mixed hardwood forest: the former longleaf pine forest. In: Biodiversity of the southeastern United States/lowland terrestrial communities. W. H. Martin, S. G. Boyce and A. C. Echternacht, eds. John Wiley and Sons, Inc.

Wass, M. L. 1972. A checklist of the biota of lower Chesapeake Bay: with inclusions from the Upper Bay and the Virginia sea. Special Scientific Report No. 65. Virginia Institute of Marine Science, Gloucester Point, VA.

Watson, R. J. 1959. The 1959 VSO annual meeting. Raven 30(3 & 4): 23–25.

Watts, B. D. 2001. Review of the avian community within Colonial National Historical Park. Center for Conservation Biology Technical Report CCBTR-01-05, College of William and Mary: 21 pp.

Watts, B. D. 2001. Review of the avian community within Colonial National Historical Park. Center for Conservation Biology Technical Report CCBTR-01-05, College of William and Mary: 21 pp.

Watts, B, D. 2003. Bird mortality associated with highway median plantings. Raven 74(2): 11–12.

Watts, B. D. and M. A. Byrd. 2002. Virginia Bald Eagle breeding survey: a twenty-five year summary (1977–2001). Raven 73(1): 3–9.

Watts, B. D. and M. A. Byrd. 2011. Virginia bald eagle nest and productivity survey: Year 2011 report. Center for Conservation Biology Technical Report Series, CCBTR-11-11. College of William and Mary, Williamsburg, VA. 42 pp.

Watts, B. D., M. A. Byrd and M. U. Watts. 1996. Status and distribution of Cliff Swallows in coastal Virginia. Raven 67(1): 21–24.

Watts, B. D., M. A. Byrd and M. U. Watts. 2004. Status and distribution of breeding Ospreys in the Chesapeake Bay: 1995–96. Journal of Raptor Research 38(1): 47–54.

Watts, B. D., Mojica, E.K. and Padgett, S. M. 2008. Virginia Peregrine Falcon monitoring and management program:,Year 2008 report. Center for Conservation Biology Technical Report Series, CCBTR-08-02. College of William and Mary, Williamsburg, VA. 19 pp.

Watts, B. D. and B. J. Paxton. 2000. The influence of thorny elaeagnus on automobile-induced bird mortality. Center for Conservation Biology Technical Report Series: CCB-TR-00-09. College of William and Mary, Williamsburg, VA. 18 pp.

Weiss, V. 2003. Nest sites used by Brown-headed Nuthatches in the Virginia Coastal Plain. Raven 74(1): 3–10.

Williams, B. 1974. Ringed Turtle Doves nesting near Williamsburg. Raven 45(2): 39–40.

Williams, B. 1988. Kites and Tails. Raven 59: 35–37.

Williams, B. 1991. Ash-throated Flycatcher near Williamsburg. Raven 62(1): 13–14.

Williams, B. 1998. The first record of the Shiny Cowbird for Virginia. Raven 69(1): 34–38.

# Index to Bird Species

119

121

# Picture Credits

Photographs used to enhance this publication were contributed by

Fred Blystone

Felice Bond

Inge Curtis

Barbara Houston

Seig Kopinitz

Mike Millen

Joe Piotrowski

Mike Powell

Brian Taber

Bill Williams

All of the pictures in this book were taken within the Colonial Historic Triangle.